THE
PYTHON BIBLE

3 IN 1

BY

FLORIAN DEDOV

Copyright © 2019

Copyright © 2019 Florian Dedov

Florian Dedov, Vienna

1st Edition

ASIN E-Book: B07W5XDKLG

ISBN-10 Paperback: 1089201842

ISBN-13 Paperback: 978-1089201847

This book is a 3-in-1 version of the first three volumes of The Python Bible series.

I recommend reading them in the right order, since the volumes build on top of each other.

If you think that this book has brought value to you and helped you on your programming journey, I would appreciate a quick review on Amazon.

Thank you!

1
PYTHON BIBLE
FOR BEGINNERS

FLORIAN DEDOV

THE
PYTHON BIBLE
VOLUME ONE

INTRODUCTION AND BASICS

BY

FLORIAN DEDOV

Copyright © 2019

TABLE OF CONTENT

INTRODUCTION

This book is the first part of a series that is called the Python Bible. In this series, we are going to focus on learning the Python programming language as effective as possible. The goal is to learn it smart and fast without needing to read thousands of pages. We will keep it simple and precise.

In this first book, we will introduce you to the language and learn the basics. It is for complete beginners and no programming, IT or math skills are needed to understand it. At the end, you will be able to write some simple and interesting programs and you will have the necessary basis to continue with volume two.

WHY PYTHON?

One question you might be asking yourself right now is: Why learn Python? Why not Java, C++ or Go?

First of all, a good programmer is fluent in multiple languages, so learning Python doesn't mean that you can't learn C++ or Java additionally. But second of all, Python is probably the best language to start with.

It is extremely simple in its syntax (the way the code is written) and very easy to learn. A lot of things that you need to do manually in other languages are automated in Python.

Besides that, Python's popularity is skyrocketing. According to the TIOBE-Index, Python is the third most popular language with an upward trend. But also in other rankings, you will see Python near the top.

TIOBE: https://www.tiobe.com/tiobe-index/

Also, Python is the lingua franca of machine learning. This means that it is the one language that is used the most in the areas of artificial intelligence, data science, finance etc. All these topics will be part of this Python Bible series. But since Python is a general-purpose language, the fields of application are numerous.

Last but not least, Python is a very good choice because of its community. Whenever you have some problem or some error in your code, you can go online and find a solution. The community is huge and everything was probably already solved by someone else.

HOW TO READ THIS BOOK

In order to get as much value as possible from this book, it is very important that you code the individual examples yourself. When you read and understand a new concept, play around with it. Write some scripts and experiment around. That's how you learn and grow.

So, stay motivated. Get excited and enjoy your programing journey. If you follow the steps in this book, you will have a solid basis and a decent understanding of the Python language. I wish you a lot of fun and success with your code!

Just one little thing before we start. This book was written for you, so that you can get as much value as possible and learn to code effectively. If you find this book valuable or you think you learned something new, please write a quick review on Amazon. It is completely free and takes about one minute. But it helps me produce more high quality books, which you can benefit from.

Thank you!

1 – INSTALLING PYTHON

Now, before we get into the code, we need to install Python and our development environment. Python is a so-called *interpreted* language. This means that the code needs a certain software (the interpreter) to be executed.

Other languages like C++ or Java are *compiled* languages. You need a compiler but then the program is converted into machine code and can be executed without extra software. Python scripts can't be executed without a Python interpreter.

PYTHON INSTALLATION

First of all, you need to visit the official Python website in order to get the latest version from there.

Python: https://www.python.org/downloads/

Download the installer and follow the instructions. Once you are done, you should have the Python interpreter as well as the IDLE on your computer.

The IDLE is an *Integrated Development and Learning Environment*. It is the basic editor, where we can write and execute our code. Just open your start menu and look for it.

Development Environment

Python IDLE

When it comes to our development environment, we have many options to choose from. The simplest choice is to just use the default IDLE. It is a great tool for writing the code and it has an integrated interpreter. So, you can execute the code directly in the IDLE. For beginners this is definitely enough. If you choose this option, you can just stick with the basic installation. In this book, we are going to assume that you are using the IDLE.

Editor and CLI

If you prefer to use a specific editor, like Atom, Sublime or VS Code, you can run your code directly from the command line. So you basically write your code in your editor and save the file. Then you run CMD (on Windows) or Terminal (on Linux & Mac). You need to use the following syntax in order to run the code:

```
python <scriptname>.py
```

This option is a bit less convenient but if you prefer using a specific editor, you may need to do it. Another way would be to look for some Python interpreter plugins for your editor.

Atom Editor: https://atom.io/

Sublime Text: https://www.sublimetext.com/

VS Code: https://code.visualstudio.com/

PYCHARM

Last but not least, you can also decide to use a very professional IDE with a lot of features. For Python this is PyCharm. This development environment is a product of JetBrains, a very well-known and professional company. It has a ton of features, professional syntax highlighting and a great user interface. I would definitely recommend it to every Python developer, but I think it might be a bit too much and not necessary for beginners. But that is your decision. If you are interested, you can get the community edition for free.

PyCharm: https://www.jetbrains.com/pycharm/

Now, let's get into the code!

2 – OUR FIRST PROGRAM

In order to understand the syntax of Python, we are going to start with a very simple first program. It is a tradition in programming to start with a *Hello World* application, when you are learning a new language. So, we are going to do that in this chapter.

HELLO WORLD

A *Hello World* application is just a script that outputs the text *"Hello World!"* onto the screen. In Python this is especially simple.

```
print("Hello World!")
```

As you can see, this is a one-liner in Python. In other languages, we would have to define a basic structure with functions, classes and more, just to print one text.

But let's see what's happening here. The first thing that we can notice is the so-called *function* with the name *print*. When we use that function, it outputs a certain text onto the screen. The text that we want to print needs to be put between the parentheses.

Another thing that is very important here, are the quotation marks. They indicate that the text is a *string* and not a name of something else. A string is a data-type that represents text. When we don't use quotation marks, the interpreter will think that *Hello World!* is a variable name and not a text. Therefore, we will get an error message. But we will talk about variables and data types in the next chapter.

RUNNING THE SCRIPT

Now, we just need to run the script we just wrote. For that, you need to save the script into a Python file. Then you can use the integrated interpreter of the IDLE. Just click on Run -> Run Module (or F5).

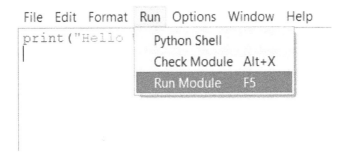

Running Code in Python IDLE

You will then see the results on the screen. That's how you run your first program.

3 – VARIABLES AND DATA TYPES

Probably, you have already encountered variables in your math classes. Basically, they are just placeholders for values. In programming, that's the same. The difference is that we have a lot of different data types, and variables cannot only store values of numbers but even of whole objects.

In this chapter we are going to take a look at variables in Python and the differences of the individual data types. Also, we will talk about type conversions.

NUMERICAL DATA TYPES

The types you probably already know from mathematics are numerical data types. There are different kinds of numbers that can be used for mathematical operations.

NUMERICAL DATA TYPES		
DATA TYPE	KEYWORD	DESCRIPTION
Integer	int	A whole number
Float	float	A floating point number
Complex	complex	A complex number

As you can see, it's quite simple. An integer is just a regular whole number, which we can do basic calculations with. A float extends the integer and allows decimal places because it is a floating point number. And a complex number is what just a number that has a *real* and an *imaginary* component. If you don't understand complex numbers mathematically, forget about them. You don't need them for your programming right now.

STRINGS

A string is just a basic sequence of characters or basically a text. Our text that we printed in the last chapter was a string. Strings always need to be surrounded by quotation marks. Otherwise the interpreter will not realize that they are meant to be treated like text. The keyword for String in Python is *str*.

BOOLEANS

Booleans are probably the most simple data type in Python. They can only have one of two values, namely *True* or *False*. It's a binary data type. We will use it a lot when we get to conditions and loops. The keyword here is *bool*.

SEQUENCES

Sequences are a topic that we will cover in a later chapter. But since sequences are also data types we will at least mention that they exist.

SEQUENCE TYPES		
DATA TYPE	**KEYWORD**	**DESCRIPTION**
List	list	Collection of values
Tuple	tuple	Immutable list
Dictionary	dict	List of key-value pairs

CREATING VARIABLES

Creating variables in Python is very simple. We just choose a name and assign a value.

```
myNumber = 10
myText = "Hello"
```

Here, we defined two variables. The first one is an integer and the second one a string. You can basically choose whatever name you want but there are some limitations. For example you are not allowed to use reserved keywords like *int* or *dict*. Also, the name is not allowed to start with a number or a special character other than the underline.

USING VARIABLES

Now that we have defined our variables, we can start to use them. For example, we could print the values.

```
print(myNumber)
print(myText)
```

Since we are not using quotation marks, the text in the parentheses is treated like a variable name.

Therefore, the interpreter prints out the values *10* and *"Hello"*.

TYPECASTING

Sometimes, we will get a value in a data type that we can't work with properly. For example we might get a string as an input but that string contains a number as its value. In this case *"10"* is not the same as *10*. We can't do calculations with a string, even if the text represents a number. For that reason we need to typecast.

```
value = "10"
number = int(value)
```

Typecasting is done by using the specific data type function. In this case we are converting a string to an integer by using the *int* keyword. You can also reverse this by using the *str* keyword. This is a very important thing and we will need it quite often.

4 – Operators

The next thing we are going to learn is operators. We use operators in order to manage variables or values and perform operations on them. There are many different types of operators and in this chapter we are going to talk about the differences and applications.

Arithmetic Operators

The simplest operators are arithmetic operators. You probably already know them from mathematics.

ARITHMETIC OPERATORS		
OPERATOR	**NAME**	**DESCRIPTION**
+	Addition	Adds two values
-	Subtraction	Subtracts one value from another
*	Multiplication	Multiplies two values
/	Division	Divides one value by another
%	Modulus	Returns the remainder of a division
**	Exponent	Takes a value to the power of another value
//	Floor Division	Returns the result of a division without decimal places

Let's take a look at some examples.

20 + 10 = 30   20 - 10 = 10

2 * 10 = 20   5 / 2 = 2.5

5 % 2 = 1   5 ** 2 = 25

5 // 2 = 2

If you don't get it right away, don't worry. Just play around with the operators and print the results. Of course you can also use variables and not only pure values.

ASSIGNMENT OPERATORS

Another type of operators we already know is assignment operators. As the name already tells us, we use them to assign values to variables.

ASSIGNMENT OPERATORS	
OPERATOR	DESCRIPTION
=	Assigns a value to a variable
+=	Adds a value to a variable
-=	Subtracts a value from a variable
*=	Multiplies a value with a variable
/=	Divides the variable by a value
%=	Assigns the remainder of a division
**=	Assigns the result of a exponentiation
//=	Assigns the result of a floor division

Basically we use these operators to directly assign a value. The two statements down below have the same effect. It's just a simpler way to write it.

```
a = a + 10
a += 10
```

COMPARISON OPERATORS

When we use comparison operators in order to compare two objects, we always get a Boolean. So our result is binary, either True or False.

COMPARISON OPERATORS		
OPERATOR	**NAME**	**DESCRIPTION**
==	Equal	Two values are the same
!=	Not Equal	Two values are not the same
>	Greater Than	One value is greater than the other
<	Less Than	One value is less than the other
>=	Greater or Equal	One value is greater than or equal to another
<=	Less or Equal	One value is less than or equal to another

We use comparisons, when we are dealing with conditions and loops. These are two topics that we will cover in later chapters.

When a comparison is right, it returns True, otherwise it returns False. Let's look at some examples.

10 == 10 → **True**   10 != 10 → **False**

20 > 10 → **True**   20 > 20 → **False**

20 >= 20 → **True**   20 < 10 → **False**

10 <= 5 → **False**

LOGICAL OPERATORS

Logical operators are used to combine or connect Booleans or comparisons.

LOGICAL OPERATORS	
OPERATOR	**DESCRIPTION**
or	At least one has to be *True*
and	Both have to be *True*
not	Negates the input

I think this is best explained by examples, so let's look at some.

True or **True** → **True**   **True** and **True** → **True**

True or **False** → **True**   **False** and **False** → **False**

False or **False** → **False**   not **True** → **False**

True and **False** → **False**   not **False** → **True**

OTHER OPERATORS

There are also other operators like bitwise or membership operators. But some of them we just don't need and others need a bit more programming knowledge to be understood. So for this chapter we will stick with those.

5 – USER INPUT

Up until now, the only thing we did is to print out text onto the screen. But what we can also do is to input our own data into the script. In this chapter, we are going to take a look at user input and how to handle it.

INPUT FUNCTION

In Python we have the function *input*, which allows us to get the user input from the console application.

```
name = input("Please enter your name:")
print(name)
```

Here, the user can input his name and it gets saved into the variable *name*. We can then call this variable and print it.

```
number1 = input("Enter first number: ")
number2 = input("Enter second number: ")
sum = number1 + number2
print("Result: ", sum)
```

This example is a bit misleading. It seems like we are taking two numbers as an input and printing the sum. The problem is that the function *input* always returns a string. So when you enter 10, the value of the variable is *"10"*, it's a string.

So, what happens when we add two strings? We just append one to the other. This means that the sum of

"15" and "26" would be "1526". If we want a mathematical addition, we need to typecast our variables first.

```
number1 = input("Enter first number: ")
number2 = input("Enter second number: ")
number1 = int(number1)
number2 = int(number2)
sum = number1 + number2
print("Result: ", sum)
```

Now our script works well! Always remember that the input function returns a string and you need to typecast it, if you want to do calculations with it.

6 – CONDITIONS

This chapter is about a concept that will make our scripts more interesting. So far, the interpreter always executed one command after the other. With conditions, this changes.

IF, ELIF, ELSE

Basically, a condition needs to return *True*, so that our script continues with the code in its block.

```
number = input("Enter a number:")
number = int(number)

if number < 10:
    print("Your number is less than 10")
elif number > 10:
    print("Your number is greater than 10")
else:
    print("Your number is 10")
```

The three important keywords here are *if, elif* and *else*. In this script, the user inputs a number that gets converted into an integer. Then our first *if-statement* checks if this number is less than ten. Remember that comparisons always return *True* or *False*. If the return is *True*, the code that is indented here gets executed. We use colons and indentations to mark code blocks in Python.

If this condition returns *False*, it continues to the *elif-block* and checks if this condition is met. The same procedure happens here. You can have as many *elif-blocks* as you want. If no condition is met, we get into the *else-block*.

FLOWCHART

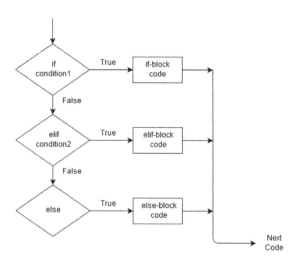

In this flowchart you can see how these basic if, elif and else trees work. Of course, you don't need an elif or else block. You can just write an if-statement and if the condition is not met, it skips the code and continues with the rest of the script.

NESTED IF-STATEMENTS

You can also put if-blocks into if-blocks. These are called *nested* if-statements.

```python
if number % 2 == 0:
    if number == 0:
        print("Your number is even but
zero")
    else:
        print("Your number is even")
else:
    print("Your number is odd")
```

So, here we have the first condition, which checks if the number is even. When it's even it then checks if it's a zero or not. That's a trivial example but you get the concept.

7 – LOOPS

If we want to automate a repetitive process, we can use loops to do that. A loop is a programming structure that executes the same code over and over again, as long as a certain condition is met. This is at least true for the classic *while loop*.

WHILE LOOP

There are two types of loops in Python: *while loops* and *for loops*. A while loop executes the code in its block *while* a condition is met.

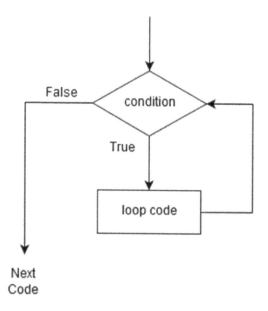

As you can see, it goes in circles until the condition returns *False*. Let's have a look at the code.

```
number = 0
while number < 10:
    number += 1
    print(number)
```

We use the *while* keyword to define the loop. Then we state a condition and again the code block is indented after the colon. In this example, we are counting from one to ten. We are initializing the variable *number* with the value zero. In every iteration, we increase it by one and print its value. This is done as long as the number is less than ten.

ENDLESS LOOP

With this knowledge, we can create an endless loop. This might seem useless but in fact it has some applications.

```
while True:
    print("This will print forever")
```

It is done by defining a loop which has the condition *True*. Since it is always *True*, the loop will never end, unless we terminate the script.

Warning: This might overload your computer, especially if it is a slow one.

FOR LOOP

The *for loop* works a bit differently. Here we don't have a condition. This loop type is used to iterate over sequences. Since these are the topic of the next chapter, we won't get into too much detail here.

```
numbers = [10, 20, 30, 40]
for number in numbers:
    print(number)
```

For now, we won't care about the syntax of sequences. Just notice that we have a list of four numbers. We then use the *for* keyword to iterate over it. The control variable *number* always gets assigned the value of the next element. In this case, we print out all the numbers.

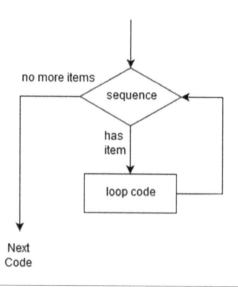

As you can see, the loop continues as long as there is a next element in the list.

Range Function

With the *range* function, we can create lists that contain all numbers in between two numbers.

```
for x in range(100):
    print(x)
```

This right here is a simple way to print all the numbers up to 100. But what you can also do is start counting from another number.

```
for x in range (20, 80):
    print(x)
```

Our range list here contains the numbers between 20 and 80.

Loop Control Statements

In order to manage loops, we have so-called *loop control statements*. They allow us to manipulate the process flow of the loop at a specific point.

Break Statement

With the *break* statement, we can end a loop immediately, without caring about the condition.

```
number = 0
while number < 10:
    number += 1
    if number == 5:
        break
    print(number)
```

Here, we have a simple counting loop. As soon as the number reaches the value five, we execute a break statement and the script continues with the rest of the code.

CONTINUE STATEMENT

If we don't want to break the full loop, but to skip only one iteration, we can use the *continue* statement.

```
number = 0
while number < 10:
    number += 1
    if number == 5:
        continue
    print(number)
```

In this example, we always increase the number by one and then print it. But if the number is a five, we skip the iteration, after the increment. So, this number doesn't get printed.

PASS STATEMENT

The *pass* statement is a very special statement, since it does absolutely nothing. Actually, it is not really a loop control statement, but a placeholder for code.

```
if number == 10:
    pass
else:
    pass

while number < 10:
    pass
```

Sometimes you want to write your basic code structure, without implementing the logic yet. In this case, we can use the pass statement, in order to fill the code blocks. Otherwise, we can't run the script.

8 – SEQUENCES

The sequence is the most basic data structure in Python. It contains multiple elements and they are indexed with a specific number. In this chapter, we are going to talk about the different types of sequences and their functions.

LISTS

The first sequence type we are looking at is the list. It is what the name says – just a list.

```
numbers = [10, 22, 6, 1, 29]
```

In Python, we define lists by using square brackets. We put the elements in between of those and separate them by commas. The elements of a list can have any data type and we can also mix them.

```
numbers = [10, 22, 6, 1, 29]
names = ["John", "Alex", "Bob"]
mixed = ["Anna", 20, 28.12, True]
```

ACCESSING VALUES

In order to access values of a sequence, we need to first talk about indices. The index is more or less the position of the element. What's important here is that we start counting from zero. So the first element has the index zero, the second has the index one and so on. We can then access the element by using the index.

```
print(numbers[2])
print(mixed[1])
print(names[0])
```

We print the third element of *numbers* (6), the second element of *names* (Alex) and the first element of *mixed* (Anna).

But instead of only accessing one single element, we can also define a range that we want to access.

```
print(numbers[1:3])  # 22 and 6
print(numbers[:3])   # 10, 22 and 6
print(numbers[1:])   # 22, 6, 1 and 29
```

By using the colon, we can slice our lists and access multiple elements at once.

MODIFYING ELEMENTS

In a list, we can also modify the values. For this, we index the elements in the same way.

```
numbers[1] = 10
names[2] = "Jack"
```

The second element of the numbers list is now *10* instead of *22* and the third element of the names list is *Jack* instead of *Bob*.

LIST OPERATIONS

Some of the operators we already know can be used when working with lists – addition and multiplication.

LIST OPERATIONS	
OPERATION	**RESULT**
[10, 20, 30] + [40, 50, 60]	[10, 20, 30, 40, 50, 60]
[10, "Bob"] * 3	[10, "Bob", 10, "Bob", 10, "Bob"]

LIST FUNCTIONS

When it comes to lists, there are a lot of different functions and methods that we can use. We are not going to talk about all of them, since it's just not necessary. Our focus will lie on the most important ones.

LIST FUNCTIONS	
FUNCTION	**DESCRIPTION**
len(list)	Returns the length of a list
max(list)	Returns the item with maximum value
min(list)	Returns the item with minimum value
list(element)	Typecasts element into list

LIST METHODS	
METHOD	**DESCRIPTION**
list.append(x)	Appends element to the list

list.count(x)	Counts how many times an element appears in the list
list.index(x)	Returns the first index at which the given element occurs
list.pop()	Removes and returns last element
list.reverse()	Reverses the order of the elements
list.sort()	Sorts the elements of a list

TUPLES

The next sequence type we are going to look at is very similar to the list. It's the *tuple*. The only difference between a list and a tuple is that a tuple is immutable. We can't manipulate it.

```
tpl = (10, 20, 30)
```

Notice that a tuple is defined by using parentheses rather than square brackets.

TUPLE FUNCTIONS

Basically, all the reading and accessing functions like *len, min* and *max* stay the same and can be used with tuples. But of course it is not possible to use any modifying or appending functions.

DICTIONARIES

The last sequence type in this chapter will be the *dictionary*. A dictionary works a bit like a lexicon. One element in this data structure points to another. We are talking about key-value pairs. Every entry in this sequence has a key and a respective value. In other programming languages this structure is called *hash map*.

```
dct = {"Name": "John",
       "Age": 25,
       "Height": 6.1}
```

We define dictionaries by using curly brackets and the key-value pairs are separated by commas. The key and the value themselves are separated by colons. On the left side there is the key and on the right side the according value.

Since the key now replaces the index, it has to be unique. This is not the case for the values. We can have many keys with the same value but when we address a certain key, it has to be the only one with that particular name. Also keys can't be changed.

ACCESSING VALUES

In order to access values of a dictionary, we need to address the keys.

```
print(dct["Name"])
print(dct["Age"])
print(dct["Height"])
```

Notice that if there were multiple keys with the same name, we couldn't get a result because we wouldn't know which value we are talking about.

DICTIONARY FUNCTIONS

Similar to lists, dictionaries also have a lot of functions and methods. But since they work a bit differently and they don't have indices, their functions are not the same.

DICTIONARY FUNCTIONS	
FUNCTION	**DESCRIPTION**
len(dict)	Returns the length of a dictionary
str(dict)	Returns the dictionary displayed as a string

DICTIONARY METHODS	
METHOD	**DESCRIPTION**
dict.clear()	Removes all elements from a dictionary
dict.copy()	Returns a copy of the dictionary
dict.fromkeys()	Returns a new dictionary with the same keys but empty values
dict.get(key)	Returns the value of the given key

dict.has_key(key)	Returns if the dictionary has a certain key or not
dict.items()	Returns all the items in a list of tuples
dict.keys()	Returns a list of all the keys
dict.update(dict2)	Add the content of another dictionary to an existing one
dict.values()	Returns a list of all the values

MEMBERSHIP OPERATORS

One type of operators we haven't talked about yet is membership operators. These are very important when it comes to sequences. We use them to check if an element is a member of a sequence, but also to iterate over sequences.

```
list1 = [10, 20, 30, 40, 50]
print(20 in list1)      # True
print(60 in list1)      # False
print(60 not in list1)  # True
```

With the *in* or *not in* operators, we check if a sequence contains a certain element. If the element is in the list, it returns *True*. Otherwise it returns *False*.

But we also use membership operators, when we iterate over sequences with for loops.

```
for x in list1:
    print(x)
```

For every element *in* the sequence *x* becomes the value of the next element and gets printed. We already talked about that in the loops chapter.

9 – FUNCTIONS

Oftentimes in programming, we implement code that we want to use over and over again at different places. That code might become quite large. Instead of re-writing it everywhere we need it, we can use *functions*.

Functions can be seen as blocks of organized code that we reuse at different places in our scripts. They make our code more modular and increase the reusability.

DEFINING FUNCTIONS

In order to define a function in Python, we use the *def* keyword, followed by a function name and parentheses. The code needs to be indented after the colon.

```python
def hello():
    print("Hello")
```

Here we have a function *hello* that prints the text *"Hello"*. It's quite simple. Now we can call the function by using its name.

```python
hello()
```

PARAMETERS

If we want to make our functions more dynamic, we can define parameters. These parameters can then be processed in the function code.

```
def print_sum(number1, number2):
    print(number1 + number2)
```

As you can see, we have two parameters in between the parentheses – *number1* and *number2.* The function *print_sum* now prints the sum of these two values.

```
print_sum(20, 30)
```

This function call prints the value *50* out onto the screen.

RETURN VALUES

The two functions we wrote were just executing statements. What we can also do is return a certain value. This value can then be saved in a variable or it can be processed. For this, use the keyword *return*.

```
def add(number1, number2):
    return number1 + number2
```

Here we return the sum of the two parameters instead of printing it. But we can then use this result in our code.

```
number3 = add(10, 20)
print(add(10, 20))
```

DEFAULT PARAMETERS

Sometimes we want our parameters to have default values in case we don't specify anything else. We can do that by assigning values in the function definition.

```python
def say(text="Default Text"):
    print(text)
```

In this case, our function *say* prints the text that we pass as a parameter. But if we don't pass anything, it prints the default text.

VARIABLE PARAMETERS

Sometimes we want our functions to have a variable amount of parameters. For that, we use the *asterisk symbol* (*) in our parameters. We then treat the parameter as a sequence.

```python
def print_sum(*numbers):
    result = 0
    for x in numbers:
        result += x
    print(result)
```

Here we pass the parameter *numbers*. That may be five, ten or a hundred numbers. We then iterate over this parameter, add every value to our sum and print it.

```python
print_sum(10, 20, 30, 40)
```

SCOPES

The last thing we are going to talk about in this chapter is *scopes*. Scopes are not only important for functions but also for loops, conditions and other structures. Basically, we need to realize the difference between local and global variables.

```python
def function():
    number = 10
    print(number)

print(number) # Doesn't work
```

In this example, you see why it's important. When you define a variable inside of a function, a loop, a condition or anything similar, this variable can't be accessed outside of that structure. It doesn't exist.

```python
number = 10

def function():
    print(number)
```

This on the other hand works. The variable *number* was defined outside of the function, so it can be *seen* inside the function. But you will notice that you can't manipulate it.

In order to manipulate an object that was defined outside of the function, we need to define it as *global*.

```python
number = 10

def function():
```

```
global number
number += 10
print(number)
```

By using the keyword *global* we can fully access and manipulate the variable.

10 – EXCEPTION HANDLING

Programming is full of errors and exceptions. If you coded along while reading and experimented around a little bit, you may have encountered one or two error messages. These errors can also be called *exceptions*. They terminate our script and crash the program if they are not handled properly.

```
result = 10 / 0

Traceback (most recent call last):
  File "<pyshell#0>", line 1, in <module>
    10 / 0
ZeroDivisionError: division by zero
```

Just try to divide a number by zero and you will get a *ZeroDivisionError*. That's because a division by zero is not defined and our script doesn't know how to handle it. So it crashes.

```
text = "Hello"
number = int(text)

Traceback (most recent call last):
  File "<pyshell#2>", line 1, in <module>
    number = int(text)
ValueError: invalid literal for int() with base 10: 'Hello'
```

Alternatively, try to typecast an ordinary text into a number. You will get a *ValueError* and the script crashes again.

TRY EXCEPT

We can handle these errors or exceptions by defining *try* and *except* blocks.

```
try:
    print(10 / 0)
    text = "Hello"
    number = int(text)
except ValueError:
    print("Code for ValueError...")
except ZeroDivisionError:
    print("Code vor ZDE...")
except:
    print("Code for other exceptions...")
```

In the *try* block we put the code that we want to execute and where errors might occur. Then we define *except* blocks that tell our script what to do in case of the respective errors. Instead of crashing, we provide code that handles the situation. This might be a simple error message or a complex algorithm.

Here we defined two specific *except* blocks for the *ValueError* and the *ZeroDivisionError*. But we also defined a general *except* block in case we get an error that doesn't fit these two types.

ELSE STATEMENTS

We can also use else statements for code that gets executed if nothing went wrong.

```python
try:
    print(10 / 0)
except:
    print("Error!")
else:
    print("Everything OK!")
```

FINALLY STATEMENTS

If we have some code that shall be executed at the end no matter what happened, we can write it into a *finally* block. This code will always be executed, even if an exception remains unhandled.

```python
try:
    print(10 / 0)
except:
    print("Error!")
finally:
    print("Always executed!")
```

11 – FILE OPERATIONS

Oftentimes, we will need to read data in from external files or to save data into files. In this chapter we will take a look at *file streams* and the various operations.

OPENING AND CLOSING FILES

Before we can read from or write into a file, we first need to open a *file stream*. This returns the respective file as an object and allows us to deal with it.

```
file = open("myfile.txt", "r")
```

We use the function *open* in order to open a new file stream. As a parameter we need to define the file name and the *access mode* (we will talk about that in a second). The function returns the stream and we can save it into our variable *file*.

ACCESS MODES

Whenever we open a file in Python, we use a certain access mode. An access mode is the way in which we access a file. For example *reading* or *writing*. The following table gives you a quick overview over the various access modes.

ACCESS MODE	
LETTER	**ACCESS MODE**
r	Reading
r+	Reading and Writing (No Truncating File)
rb	Reading Binary File
rb+	Reading and Writing Binary File (No Truncating File)
w	Writing
w+	Reading and Writing (Truncating File)
wb	Writing Binary File
wb+	Reading and Writing Binary File (Truncating File)
a	Appending
a+	Reading and Appending
ab	Appending Binary File
ab+	Reading and Appending Binary File

The difference between r+ or rb+ and w+ or wb+ is that w+ and wb+ overwrite existing files and create new ones if they don't exist. This is not the case for r+ and rb+.

CLOSING FILES

When we are no longer in need of our opened file stream, we should always close it. Python does this automatically in some cases but it is considered good practice to close streams manually. We close a stream by using the method *close*.

```
file = open("myfile.txt", "r+")
# CODE
file.close()
```

WITH STATEMENT

Alternatively, we can open and close streams more effectively by using *with* statements. A *with* statement opens a stream, executes the indented code and closes the stream afterwards.

```
with open("myfile.txt", "r") as file:
    # Some Code
```

It shortens the code and makes it easier to not forget to close your streams.

READING FROM FILES

Once we have opened a file in a reading mode, we can start reading its content. For this, we use the *read* method.

```
file = open('myfile.txt', 'r')
print(file.read())
file.close()
```

Here we open the file in reading mode and then print out its content. We can do the same thing by using the *with* statement.

```
with open('myfile.txt', 'r') as file:
    print(file.read())
```

But we don't have to read the whole file, if we don't want to. We can also read the first 20 or 50 characters by passing a parameter to the method.

```
with open('myfile.txt', 'r') as file:
    print(file.read(50))
```

WRITING INTO FILES

When we write into a file, we need to ask ourselves if we just want to add our text or if we want to completely overwrite a file. So we need to choose between writing and appending mode. For writing in general we use the method *write*.

```
file = open('myfile.txt', 'w')
print(file.write("Hello File!"))
file.flush()
file.close()
```

We open our file in writing mode and write our little text into the file. Notice that the text doesn't get written until we *flush* the stream. In this case this is not necessary because when we close a stream it flushes automatically. Let's look at the *with* statement alternative again.

```
with open('myfile.txt', 'w') as file:
    print(file.write("Hello File!"))
```

If we want to append our text, we just have to change the access mode. Everything else stays the same.

```
with open('myfile.txt', 'a') as file:
    print(file.write("Hello File!"))
```

OTHER OPERATIONS

Now if we want to perform other operations than writing, reading and appending, we will need to import and extra module. The basic Python functions and classes are available by default. But many things like mathematics, networking, threading and also additional file operations, require the import of modules. In this case we need to import the *os* module, which stands for operating system.

```
import os
```

This would be one way to import this module. But if we do it like that, we would always need to specify the module when we use a function. To make it easier for us, we will do it like that.

```
from os import *
```

Basically, what we are saying here is: Import all the function and classes from the module *os*. Notice that the import statements of a script should always be the first thing at the top.

DELETING AND RENAMING

For deleting and renaming files we have two very simple functions from the *os* module – *remove* and *rename*.

```
remove("myfile.txt")
rename("myfile.txt", "newfile.txt")
```

We can also use the *rename* function, to move files into different directories. But the directory has to already be there. This function can't create new directories.

```
rename("myfile.txt", "newdir/myfile.txt")
```

DIRECTORY OPERATIONS

With the *os* module we can also operate with directories. We can create, delete and navigate through them.

```
mkdir("newdir")
chdir("newdir")
chdir("..")
rmdir("newdir")
```

Here we create a new directory by using the *mkdir* (make directory) function. We then go into that directory with the *chdir (change directory)* function and then back to the previous directory with the same function. Last but not least we remove the directory with the *rmdir (remove directory)* function.

By using *("..")* we navigate back one directory. Additionally, if we would want to specify a whole path like "C:\Users\Python\Desktop\file.txt", we would have to use double backslashes since Python uses single backslashes for different purposes. But we will talk about this in the next chapter in more detail.

12 – String Functions

Even though strings are just texts or sequences of characters, we can apply a lot of functions and operations on them. Since this is a book for beginners, we won't get too much into the details here, but it is important for you to know how to deal with strings properly.

Strings as Sequences

As I already said, strings are sequences of characters and they can also be treated like that. We can basically index and slice the individual characters.

```
text = "Hello World!"
print(text[:5])
print(text[6:11])
```

The first slice we print is *"Hello"* and the second one is *"World"*. Another thing we can do is to iterate over strings with for loops.

```
text = "Hello World!"
for x in text:
    print(x)
```

In this example, we print the individual characters one after the other.

Escape Characters

In strings we can use a lot of different *escape characters*. These are non-printable characters like *tab* or *new line*. They are all initiated by a backslash, which is the reason why we need to use double backslashes for file paths (see last chapter).

The following table summarizes the most important of these escape characters. If you are interested in all the other ones just use google but you won't need them for now.

ESCAPE CHARATCERS	
NOTATION	**DESCRIPTION**
\b	Backspace
\n	New Line
\s	Space
\t	Tab

STRING FORMATTING

When we have a text which shall include the values of variables, we can use the % operator and placeholders, in order to insert our values.

```
name, age = "John", 25
print("%s is my name!" % name)
print("I am %d years old!" % age)
```

Notice that we used different placeholders for different data types. We use *%s* for strings and *%d* for integers. The following table shows you which placeholders are needed for which data types.

PLACEHOLDERS	
PLACEHOLDER	**DATA TYPE**
%c	Character
%s	String
%d or %i	Integer
%f	Float
%e	Exponential Notation

If you want to do it more general without specifying data types, you can use the *format* function.

```
name, age = "John", 25
print("My name is {} and I am {} years old"
    .format(name, age))
```

Here we use curly brackets as placeholders and insert the values afterwards using the *format* function.

STRING FUNCTIONS

There are a ton of string functions in Python and it would be unnecessary and time wasting to talk about all of them in this book. If you want an overview just go online and look for them. One website, where you can find them is W3Schools.

W3Schools Python String Functions:
https://www.w3schools.com/python/python_ref_string.asp

In this chapter however, we will focus on the most essential, most interesting and most important of these functions. The ones that you might need in the near future.

CASE MANIPULATING FUNCTIONS

We have five different case manipulating string functions in Python. Let's have a look at them.

CASE MANIPULATING FUNCTIONS	
FUNCTION	**DESCRIPTION**
string.lower()	Converts all letters to lowercase
string.upper()	Converts all letters to uppercase
string.title()	Converts all letters to titlecase
string.capitalize()	Converts first letter to uppercase
string.swapcase()	Swaps the case of all letters

COUNT FUNCTION

If you want to count how many times a specific string occurs in another string, you can use the *count* function.

```
text = "I like you and you like me!"
print(text.count("you"))
```

In this case, the number two will get printed, since the string *"you"* occurs two times.

FIND FUNCTION

In order to find the first occurrence of a certain string in another string, we use the *find* function.

```
text = "I like you and you like me!"
print(text.find("you"))
```

Here the result is 7 because the first occurrence of *"you"* is at the index 7.

JOIN FUNCTION

With the *join* function we can join a sequence to a string and separate each element by this particular string.

```
names = ["Mike", "John", "Anna"]
sep = "-"
print(sep.join(names))
```

The result looks like this: Mike-John-Anna

REPLACE FUNCTION

The *replace* function replaces one string within a text by another one. In the following example, we replace the name *John* by the name *Anna*.

```
text = "I like John and John is my friend!"
text = text.replace("John", "Anna")
```

Split Function

If we want to split specific parts of a string and put them into a list, we use the *split* function.

```
names = "John,Max,Bob,Anna"
name_list = names.split(",")
```

Here we have a string of names separated by commas. We then use the *split* function and define the comma as the separator in order to save the individual names into a list.

Triple Quotes

The last topic of this chapter is *triple quotes*. They are just a way to write multi-line strings without the need of escape characters.

```
print('''Hello World!
This is a multi-line comment!

And we don't need to use escape characters
in order to write new empty lines!''')
```

WHAT'S NEXT?

You made it! We covered all of the core basics of Pythons. You now understand how this language is structured but also general programming principles like conditions, loops and functions. Definitely, you are now able to develop a basic calculator or other simple applications. But the journey has just begun.

This is only the first part of the Python Bible Series. We've covered the topics for beginners but the real fun starts when we get into more advanced topics like network programming, threading, machine learning, data science, finance, neural networks and more. With this book you have an excellent basis for the next volumes of the Python Bible and I encourage you to continue your journey.

The next part will be for intermediates and advanced programmers, which you know belong to. So stay tuned and keep coding!

Last but not least, a little reminder. This book was written for you, so that you can get as much value as possible and learn to code effectively. If you find this book valuable or you think you learned something new, please write a quick review on Amazon. It is completely free and takes about one minute. But it helps me produce more high quality books, which you can benefit from.

Thank you!

2

PYTHON
BIBLE

FOR INTERMEDIATES

FLORIAN DEDOV

THE
PYTHON BIBLE
VOLUME TWO

INTERMEDIATE AND ADVANCED

BY

FLORIAN DEDOV

Copyright © 2019

TABLE OF CONTENT

INTRODUCTION

I think I don't have to convince you that Python is one of the most important languages of our time and worth learning. If you are reading this book, I assume that you have already programmed in Python and know the basic concepts of this language. For this book, you will definitely need the foreknowledge from the first volume, since we will build on the skills taught there.

INTERMEDIATE CONCEPTS

So what can you expect from this second volume? Basically, we will dive deep into more advanced topics of Python but also of programming in general. We'll start with object-oriented programming, classes and objects. Then we will talk about multithreading, network programming and database access. Also, we are going to build an efficient port scanner along the way. After that, we will cover recursion, XML processing and other interesting topics like logging and regular expressions.

There is a lot to learn here and the concepts get more and more complex as we go on. So stay tuned and code along while reading. This will help you to understand the material better and to practice implementing it. I wish you a lot of fun and success with your journey and this book!

Just one little thing before we start. This book was written for you, so that you can get as much value as possible and learn to code effectively. If you find this book valuable or you think you have learned something new, please write a quick review on Amazon. It is completely free and takes about one minute. But it helps me produce more high quality books, which you can benefit from.

Thank you!

1 – CLASSES AND OBJECTS

Python is an object-oriented language which means that the code can be divided into individual units, namely *objects*. Each of these objects is an instance of a so-called *class*. You can think of the class as some sort of blueprint. For example, the blueprint of a car could be the class and an object would be the actual physical car. So a class has specific attributes and functions but the values vary from object to object.

CREATING CLASSES

In Python, we use the keyword *class* in order to define a new class. Everything that is indented after the colon belongs to the class.

```
class Car:

    def __init__(self, manufacturer, model, hp):
        self.manufacturer = manufacturer
        self.model = model
        self.hp = hp
```

After the *class* keyword, we put the class name. In this example, this is *Car*.

CONSTRUCTOR

What we notice first here, is a special function called *__init__*. This is the so-called *constructor*. Every time we create an instance or an object of our class, we use this constructor. As you can see, it accepts a couple of parameters. The first one is the parameter *self* and it is mandatory. Every function of the class needs to have at least this parameter.

The other parameters are just our custom attributes. In this case, we have chosen the manufacturer, the model and the horse power (hp).

When we write *self.attribute*, we refer to the actual attribute of the respective object. We then assign the value of the parameters to it.

ADDING FUNCTIONS

We can simply add functions to our class that perform certain actions. These functions can also access the attributes of the class.

```python
class Car:

    def __init__(self, manufacturer, model, hp):
        self.manufacturer = manufacturer
        self.model = model
        self.hp = hp

    def print_info(self):
        print("Manufacturer: {}, Model: {}, HP; {}"
              .format(self.manufacturer,
                      self.model,
                      self.hp))
```

Here we have the function *print_info* that prints out information about the attributes of the respective object. Notice that we also need the parameter *self* here.

CLASS VARIABLES

In the following code, you can see that we can use one and the same variable across all the objects of the class, when it is defined without referring to *self*.

```python
class Car:

    amount_cars = 0

    def __init__(self, manufacturer, model, hp):
        self.manufacturer = manufacturer
        self.model = model
        self.hp = hp
        Car.amount_cars += 1

    def print_car_amount(self):
        print("Amount: {}"
              .format(Car.amount_cars))
```

The variable *amount_cars* doesn't belong to the individual object since it's not addressed with *self*. It is a class variable and its value is the same for all objects or instances.

Whenever we create a new car object, it increases by one. Then, every object can access and print the amount of existing cars.

DESTRUCTORS

In Python, we can also specify a method that gets called when our object gets *destroyed* or *deleted* and is no longer needed. This function is called *destructor* and it is the opposite of the *constructor*.

```python
class Car:

    amount_cars = 0

    def __init__(self, manufacturer, model, hp):
        self.manufacturer = manufacturer
        self.model = model
        self.hp = hp
        Car.amount_cars += 1

    def __del__(self):
        print("Object gets deleted!")
        Car.amount_cars -=1
```

The destructor function is called *__del__*. In this example, we print an informational message and decrease the amount of existing cars by one, when an object gets deleted.

CREATING OBJECTS

Now that we have implemented our class, we can start to create some objects of it.

```
myCar1 = Car("Tesla", "Model X", 525)
```

First, we specify the name of our object, like we do with ordinary variables. In this case, our object's name is *myCar1*. We then create an object of the *Car* class by writing the class name as a function. This calls the constructor, so we can pass our parameters. We can then use the functions of our car object.

```
myCar1.print_info()
myCar1.print_car_amount()
```

The results look like this:

```
Manufacturer: Tesla, Model: Model X, HP; 525
Amount: 1
```

What you can also do is directly access the attributes of an object.

```
print(myCar1.manufacturer)
print(myCar1.model)
print(myCar1.hp)
```

Now let's create some more cars and see how the amount changes.

```
myCar1 = Car("Tesla", "Model X", 525)
myCar2 = Car("BMW", "X3", 200)
myCar3 = Car("VW", "Golf", 100)
myCar4 = Car("Porsche", "911", 520)

del myCar3

myCar1.print_car_amount()
```

Here we first create four different car objects. We then delete one of them and finally we print out the car amount. The result is the following:

```
Object gets deleted!
Amount: 3
```

Notice that all the objects get deleted automatically when our program ends. But we can manually delete them before that happens by using the *del* keyword.

HIDDEN ATTRIBUTES

If we want to create *hidden* attributes that can only be accessed within the class, we can do this with *underlines*.

```
class MyClass:

    def __init__(self):
        self.__hidden = "Hello"
        print(self.__hidden) # Works

m1 = MyClass()
print(m1.__hidden) # Doesn't Work
```

By putting two underlines before the attribute name, we make it invisible from outside the class. The first print function works because it is inside of the class. But when we try to access this attribute from the object, we can't.

INHERITANCE

One very important and powerful concept of object-oriented programming is *inheritance*. It allows us to use existing classes and to extend them with new attributes and functions.

For example, we could have the *parent class* which represents a *Person* and then we could have many *child classes* like *Dancer, Policeman, Artist* etc. All of these would be considered a person and they would have the same basic attributes. But they are special kinds of persons with more attributes and functions.

```
class Person:

    def __init__(self, name, age):
        self.name = name
        self.age = age

    def get_older(self, years):
        self.age += years

class Programmer(Person):

    def __init__(self, name, age, language):
        super(Programmer, self).__init__(name, age)
        self.language = language

    def print_language(self):
        print("Favorite Programming Language: {}"
            .format(self.language))
```

You can see that we created two classes here. The first one is the *Person* class, which has the attributes *name* and *age*. Additionally, it has a function *get_older* that increases the age.

The second class is the *Programmer* class and it inherits from the *Person* class. This is stated in the parentheses after the class name. In the constructor we have one additional attribute *language*. First we need to pass our class to the *super* function. This function allows us to call the constructor of the parent class *Person*. There we pass our first two parameters. We also have an additional function *print_language*.

```
p1 = Programmer("Mike", 30, "Python")

print(p1.age)
print(p1.name)
print(p1.language)

p1.get_older(5)

print(p1.age)
```

Our *Programmer* object can now access all the attributes and functions of its parent class, additionally to its new values. These are the results of the statements:

```
30
Mike
Python
35
```

OVERWRITING METHODS

When one class inherits from another class, it can overwrite its methods. This is automatically done by defining a method with the same name and the same amount of parameters.

```
class Animal:

    def __init__(self, name):
        self.name = name

    def make_sound(self):
        print("Some sound!")

class Dog(Animal):

    def __init__(self, name):
        super(Dog, self).__init__(name)

    def make_sound(self):
        print("Bark!")
```

Here the function *make_sound* was overwritten in the child class *Dog*. It now has a different functionality than the function of the parent class *Animal*.

OPERATOR OVERLOADING

When we create a class with various attributes, it is not clear what should happen when we perform certain operations on them. For example, what should happen when we add two humans or when we multiply them? Since there is no default solution for this question, we can *overload* and define the operators ourselves. That allows us to choose what happens when we apply the operators on our objects.

```python
class Vector():

    def __init__(self, x, y):
        self.x = x
        self.y = y

    def __str__(self):
        return "X: %d, Y: %d" % (self.x,
                                  self.y)

    def __add__(self, other):
        return Vector(self.x + other.x,
                      self.y + other.y)

    def __sub__(self, other):
        return Vector(self.x - other.x,
                      self.y - other.y)
```

Here you see a class that represents the function of a *Vector*. When you add a vector to another, you need to add the individual values. This is the same for subtracting. If you don't know what vectors are mathematically, forget about them. This is just one example.

We use the functions __*add*__ and __*sub*__ to define what happens when we apply the + and the – operator. The __*str*__ function determines what happens when we print the object.

```
v1 = Vector(3, 5)
v2 = Vector(6, 2)
v3 = v1 + v2
v4 = v1 - v2

print(v1)
print(v2)
print(v3)
print(v4)
```

The results are the following:

```
X: 3, Y: 5
X: 6, Y: 2
X: 9, Y: 7
X: -3, Y: 3
```

2 – MULTITHREADING

Threads are lightweight processes that perform certain actions in a program and they are part of a process themselves. These threads can work in parallel with each other in the same way as two individual applications can.

Since threads in the same process share the memory space for the variables and the data, they can exchange information and communicate efficiently. Also, threads need fewer resources than processes. That's why they're often called lightweight processes.

HOW A THREAD WORKS

A thread has a beginning or a start, a working sequence and an end. But it can also be stopped or put on hold at any time. The latter is also called *sleep*.

There are two types of threads: *Kernel Threads* and *User Threads*. Kernel threads are part of the operating system, whereas user threads are managed by the programmer. That's why we will focus on user threads in this book.

In Python, a thread is a class that we can create instances of. Each of these instances then represents an individual thread which we can start, pause or stop. They are all independent from each other and they can perform different operations at the same time.

For example, in a video game, one thread could be rendering all the graphics, while another thread processes the keyboard and mouse inputs. It would be unthinkable to serially perform these tasks one after the other.

STARTING THREADS

In order to work with threads in Python, we will need to import the respective library *threading*.

```
import threading
```

Then, we need to define our target function. This will be the function that contains the code that our thread shall be executing. Let's just keep it simple for the beginning and write a *hello world* function.

```
import threading

def hello():
    print("Hello World!")

t1 = threading.Thread(target=hello)
t1.start()
```

After we have defined the function, we create our first thread. For this, we use the class *Thread* of the imported *threading* module. As a parameter, we specify the *target* to be the *hello* function. Notice that we don't put parentheses after our function name here, since we are not calling it but just referring to it. By using the *start* method we put our thread to work and it executes our function.

START VS RUN

In this example, we used the function *start* to put our thread to work. Another alternative would be the function *run*. The difference between these two functions gets important, when we are dealing with more than just one thread.

When we use the *run* function to execute our threads, they run serially one after the other. They wait for each other to finish. The *start* function puts all of them to work simultaneously.

The following example demonstrates this difference quite well.

```python
import threading

def function1():
    for x in range(1000):
        print("ONE")

def function2():
    for x in range(1000):
        print("TWO")

t1 = threading.Thread(target=function1)
t2 = threading.Thread(target=function2)
t1.start()
t2.start()
```

When you run this script, you will notice that the output alternates between *ONEs* and *TWOs*. Now if you use the *run* function instead of the *start* function, you will see 1000 times *ONE* followed by 1000 times *TWO*. This shows you that the threads are run serially and not in parallel.

One more thing that you should know is that the application itself is also the main thread, which continues to run in the background. So while your threads are running, the code of the script will be executed unless you wait for the threads to finish.

WAITING FOR THREADS

If we want to wait for our threads to finish before we move on with the code, we can use the *join* function.

```python
import threading

def function():
    for x in range(500000):
        print("HELLO WORLD!")

t1 = threading.Thread(target=function)
t1.start()

print("THIS IS THE END!")
```

If you execute this code, you will start printing the text *"HELLO WORLD!"* 500,000 times. But what you will notice is that the last print statement gets executed immediately after our thread starts and not after it ends.

```python
t1 = threading.Thread(target=function)
t1.start()

t1.join()

print("THIS IS THE END!")
```

By using the *join* function here, we wait for the thread to finish before we move on with the last print statement. If we want to set a maximum time that we want to wait, we just pass the number of seconds as a parameter.

```
t1 = threading.Thread(target=function)
t1.start()

t1.join(5)

print("THIS IS THE END!")
```

In this case, we will wait for the thread to finish but only a maximum of five seconds. After this time has passed we will proceed with the code.

Notice that we are only waiting for this particular thread. If we would have other threads running at the same time, we would have to call the *join* function on each of them in order to wait for all of them.

THREAD CLASSES

Another way to build our threads is to create a class that inherits the *Thread* class. We can then modify the *run* function and implement our functionality. The *start* function is also using the code from the *run* function so we don't have to worry about that.

```python
import threading

class MyThread(threading.Thread):

    def __init__(self, message):
        threading.Thread.__init__(self)
        self.message = message

    def run(self):
        for x in range(100):
            print(self.message)

mt1 = MyThread("This is my thread message!")
mt1.start()
```

It is basically the same but it offers more modularity and structure, if you want to use attributes and additional functions.

SYNCHRONIZING THREADS

Sometimes you are going to have multiple threads running that all try to access the same resource. This may lead to inconsistencies and problems. In order to prevent such things there is a concept called *locking*. Basically, one thread is locking all of the other threads and they can only continue to work when the lock is removed.

I came up with the following quite trivial example. It seems a bit abstract but you can still get the concept here.

```python
import threading
import time

x = 8192

def halve():
    global x
    while(x > 1):
        x /= 2
        print(x)
        time.sleep(1)
    print("END!")

def double():
    global x
    while(x < 16384):
        x *= 2
        print(x)
        time.sleep(1)
    print("END!")

t1 = threading.Thread(target=halve)
t2 = threading.Thread(target=double)

t1.start()
t2.start()
```

Here we have two functions and the variable *x* that starts at the value *8192*. The first function halves the number as long as it is greater than one, whereas the second function doubles the number as long as it is less than *16384*.

Also, I've imported the module *time* in order to use the function *sleep*. This function puts the thread to sleep for a couple of seconds (in this case one second). So it pauses. We just do that, so that we can better track what's happening.

When we now start two threads with these target functions, we will see that the script won't come to an end. The *halve* function will constantly decrease the number and the *double* function will constantly increase it.

With locking we can now let one function finish before the next function starts. Of course, in this example this is not very useful but we can do the same thing in much more complex situations.

```python
import threading
import time

x = 8192

lock = threading.Lock()

def halve():
    global x, lock
    lock.acquire()
    while(x > 1):
        x /= 2
        print(x)
        time.sleep(1)
    print("END!")
    lock.release()

def double():
    global x, lock
    lock.acquire()
    while(x < 16384):
        x *= 2
        print(x)
        time.sleep(1)
    print("END!")
    lock.release()

t1 = threading.Thread(target=halve)
t2 = threading.Thread(target=double)

t1.start()
t2.start()
```

So here we added a couple of elements. First of all we defined a *Lock* object. It is part of the *threading* module and we need this object in order to manage the locking.

Now, when we want to try to lock the resource, we use the function *acquire*. If the lock was already locked by someone else, we wait until it is released again before we continue with the code. However, if the lock is free, we lock it ourselves and release it at the end using the *release* function.

Here, we start both functions with a locking attempt. The first function that gets executed will lock the other function and finish its loop. After that it will release the lock and the other function can do the same.

So the number will be halved until it reaches the number one and then it will be doubled until it reaches the number *16384*.

SEMAPHORES

Sometimes we don't want to completely lock a resource but just limit it to a certain amount of threads or accesses. In this case, we can use so-called *semaphores*.

To demonstrate this concept, we will look at another very abstract example.

```python
import threading
import time

semaphore = threading.BoundedSemaphore(value=5)

def access(thread_number):
    print("{}: Trying access..."
          .format(thread_number))
    semaphore.acquire()
    print("{}: Access granted!"
          .format(thread_number))
    print("{}: Waiting 5 seconds..."
          .format(thread_number))
    time.sleep(5)
    semaphore.release()
    print("{}: Releasing!"
          .format(thread_number))

for thread_number in range(10):
    t = threading.Thread(target=access,
                         args=(thread_number,))
    t.start()
```

We first use the *BoundedSemaphore* class to create our *semaphore* object. The parameter *value* determines how many parallel accesses we allow. In this case, we choose five.

With our *access* function, we try to access the semaphore. Here, this is also done with the *acquire* function. If there are less than five threads utilizing the semaphore, we can acquire it and continue with the code. But when it's full, we need to wait until some other thread frees up one space.

When we run this code, you will see that the first five threads will immediately run the code, whereas the remaining five threads will need to wait five seconds until the first threads *release* the semaphore.

This process makes a lot of sense when we have limited resources or limited computational power in a system and we want to limit the access to it.

EVENTS

With *events* we can manage our threads even better. We can pause a thread and wait for a certain *event* to happen, in order to continue it.

```python
import threading

event = threading.Event()

def function():
    print("Waiting for event...")
    event.wait()
    print("Continuing!")

thread = threading.Thread(target=function)
thread.start()

x = input("Trigger event?")
if(x == "yes"):
    event.set()
```

To define an *event* we use the *Event* class of the *threading* module. Now we define our *function* which waits for our event. This is done with the *wait* function. So we start the thread and it waits.

Then we ask the user, if he wants to trigger the event. If the answer is yes, we trigger it by using the *set* function. Once the event is triggered, our function no longer waits and continues with the code.

DAEMON THREADS

So-called *daemon threads* are a special kind of thread that runs in the background. This means that the program can be terminated even if this thread is still running. Daemon threads are typically used for background tasks like synchronizing, loading or cleaning up files that are not needed anymore. We define a thread as a *daemon* by setting the respective parameter in the constructor for *Thread* to *True*.

```python
import threading
import time

path = "text.txt"
text = ""

def readFile():
    global path, text
    while True:
        with open(path) as file:
            text = file.read()
        time.sleep(3)

def printloop():
    global text
    for x in range(30):
        print(text)
        time.sleep(1)
```

```
t1 = threading.Thread(target=readFile,
daemon=True)
t2 = threading.Thread(target=printloop)

t1.start()
t2.start()
```

So, here we have two functions. The first one constantly reads in the text from a file and saves it into the *text* variable. This is done in an interval of three seconds. The second one prints out the content of *text* every second but only 30 times.

As you can see, we start the *readFile* function in a *daemon thread* and the *printloop* function in an ordinary thread. So when we run this script and change the content of the *text.txt* file while it is running, we will see that it prints the actual content all the time. Of course, we first need to create that file manually.

After it printed the content 30 times however, the whole script will stop, even though the daemon thread is still reading in the files. Since the ordinary threads are all finished, the program ends and the daemon thread just gets terminated.

3 – QUEUES

In Python, *queues* are structures that take in data in a certain order to then output it in a certain order. The default queue type is the so-called *FIFO queue*. This stands for *first in first out* and the name describes exactly what it does. The elements that enter the queue first are also the elements that will leave the queue first.

```python
import queue

q = queue.Queue()

for x in range(5):
    q.put(x)

for x in range(5):
    print(q.get(x))
```

In order to work with queues in Python, we need to import the module *queue*. We can then create an instance of the class *Queue* by using the constructor.

As you can see, we are using two functions here – *put* and *get*. The *put* function adds an element to the queue that can then be extracted by the *get* function.

Here, we put in the numbers one to five into our queue. Then, we just get the elements and print them. The order stays the same, since the default queue is *FIFO*.

QUEUING RESOURCES

Let's say we have a list of numbers that need to be processed. We decide to use multiple threads, in order to speed up the process. But there might be a problem. The threads don't know which number has already been processed and they might do the same work twice, which would be unnecessary. Also, solving the problem with a counter variable won't always work, because too many threads access the same variable and numbers might get skipped.

In this case we can just use queues to solve our problems. We fill up our queue with the numbers and every thread just uses the *get* function, to get the next number and process it.

Let's say we have the following *worker* function:

```python
import threading
import queue
import math

q = queue.Queue()
threads = []

def worker():
    while True:
        item = q.get()
        if item is None:
            break
        print(math.factorial(item))
        q.task_done()
```

We start out with an empty queue and an empty list for threads. Our function has an endless loop that gets numbers from the list and calculates the factorial of them. For this *factorial* function, we need to import the module *math*. But you can ignore this part, since it is only used because the computation requires a lot of resources and takes time. At the end, we use the function *task_done* of the queue, in order to signal that the element was processed.

```
for x in range(5):
    t = threading.Thread(target=worker)
    t.start()
    threads.append(t)

zahlen = [134000, 14, 5, 300, 98, 88, 11, 23]

for item in zahlen:
    q.put(item)

q.join()

for i in range(5):
    q.put(None)
```

We then use a for loop to create and start five threads that we also add to our list. After that, we create a list of numbers, which we then all put into the queue.

The method *join* of the *queue* waits for all elements to be extracted and processed. Basically, it waits for all the *task_done* functions. After that, we put *None* elements into the queue, so that our loops break.

Notice that our threads can't process the same element twice or even skip one because they can only get them by using the *get* function.

If we would use a counter for this task, two threads might increase it at the same time and then skip an element. Or they could just access the same element simultaneously. Queues are irreplaceable for tasks like this. We will see a quite powerful application of queues in the chapter about *networking*.

LIFO QUEUES

An alternative to the *FIFO queues* would be the *LIFO queues*. That stands for *last in first out*. You can imagine this queue like some sort of stack. The element you put last on top of the stack is the first that you can get from it.

```python
import queue

q = queue.LifoQueue()

numbers = [1, 2, 3, 4, 5]

for x in numbers:
    q.put(x)

while not q.empty():
    print(q.get())
```

By using the *LifoQueue* class from the *queue* module, we can create an instance of this type. When we now put in the numbers one to five in ascending order, we will get them back in descending order.

The result would be:

```
5 4 3 2 1
```

PRIORITIZING QUEUES

What we can also do in Python, is creating *prioritized queues*. In these, every element gets assigned a level of priority that determines when they will leave the queue.

```python
import queue

q = queue.PriorityQueue()

q.put((8, "Some string"))
q.put((1, 2023))
q.put((90, True))
q.put((2, 10.23))

while not q.empty():
    print(q.get())
```

Here, we create a new instance of the class *PriorityQueue*. When we put a new element into this queue, we need to pass a *tuple* as a parameter. The first element of the tuple is the level of importance (the lower the number, the higher the priority) and the second element is the actual object or value that we want to put into the queue.

When we execute the print statement of the loop, we get the following results:

```
(1, 2023)
(2, 10.23)
(8, 'Some string')
(90, True)
```

As you can see, the elements got sorted by their priority number. If you only want to access the actual value, you need to address the index one because it is the second value of the tuple.

```
while not q.empty():
    print(q.get()[1])
```

4 – NETWORK PROGRAMMING

Now we get into one of the most interesting intermediate topics – *network programming*. It is about communicating with other applications and devices via some network. That can be the internet or just the local area network.

SOCKETS

WHAT ARE SOCKETS?

Whenever we talk about networking in programming, we also have to talk about *sockets*. They are the endpoints of the communication channels or basically, the endpoints that talk to each other. The communication may happen in the same process or even across different continents over the internet.

What's important is that in Python we have different access levels for the network services. At the lower layers, we can access the simple sockets that allow us to use the connection-oriented and connectionless protocols like TCP or UDP, whereas other Python modules like *FTP* or *HTTP* are working on a higher layer – the *application layer*.

CREATING SOCKETS

In order to work with sockets in Python, we need to import the module *socket*.

```
import socket
```

Now, before we start defining and initializing our socket, we need to know a couple of things in advance:

- Are we using an internet socket or a UNIX socket?

- Which protocol are we going to use?

- Which IP-address are we using?

- Which port number are we using?

The first question can be answered quite simply. Since we want to communicate over a network instead of the operating system, we will stick with the *internet socket*.

The next question is a bit trickier. We choose between the protocols *TCP* (Transmission Control Protocol) and *UDP* (User Datagram Protocol). TCP is connection-oriented and more trustworthy than UDP. The chances of losing data are minimal in comparison to UDP. On the other hand, UDP is much faster than TCP. So the choice depends on the task we want to fulfil. For our examples, we will stick with

TCP since we don't care too much about speed for now.

The IP-address should be the address of the host our application will run on. For now, we will use *127.0.0.1* which is the *localhost* address. This applies to every machine. But notice that this only works when you are running your scripts locally.

For our port we can basically choose any number we want. But be careful with low numbers, since all numbers up to 1024 are *standardized* and all numbers from 1024 to 49151 are *reserved*. If you choose one of these numbers, you might have some conflicts with other applications or your operating system.

```
import socket

s = socket.socket(socket.AF_INET,
                  socket.SOCK_STREAM)
```

Here we created our first socket, by initializing an instance of the class *socket*. Notice that we passed two parameters here. The first one *AF_INET* states that we want an *internet socket* rather than a *UNIX socket*. The second one *SOCK_STREAM* is for the protocol that we choose. In this case it stands for *TCP*. If we wanted *UDP*, we would have to choose SOCK_DGRAM.

So we have a socket that uses the IP protocol (internet) and the TCP protocol. Now, before we get into the actual setup of the socket, we need to talk a little bit about clients and servers.

CLIENT-SERVER ARCHITECTURE

In a nutshell, the server is basically the one who provides information and *serves* data, whereas the clients are the ones who request and receive the data from the server.

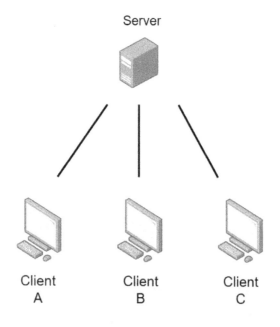

A server opens up a session with every client that connects to it. This way, servers are able to serve multiple clients at once and individually.

SERVER SOCKET METHODS

There are three methods of the *socket* class that are of high importance for the servers.

SERVER SOCKET METHODS	
METHOD	**DESCRIPTION**
bind()	Binds the address that consists of hostname and port to the socket
listen()	Waits for a message or a signal
accept()	Accepts the connection with a client

CLIENT SOCKET METHODS

For the client, there is only one specific and very important method, namely *connect*. With this method the client attempts to connect to a server which then has to *accept* this with the respective method.

OTHER SOCKET METHODS

Also, there are some other socket methods that are quite important in general.

OTHER SOCKET METHODS	
METHOD	**DESCRIPTION**
recv()	Receives a TCP message
send()	Sends a TCP message
recvfrom()	Receives a UDP message
sendto()	Sends a UDP message
close()	Closes a socket
gethostname()	Returns hostname of a socket

CREATING A SERVER

Now that we understand the client-server architecture, we are going to implement our server. We decided that we want to use TCP and an internet socket. For the address we will use the *localhost* address *127.0.0.1* and as a port, we will choose *9999*.

```
s = socket.socket(socket.AF_INET,
                  socket.SOCK_STREAM)
s.bind(("127.0.0.1", 9999))
s.listen()
print("Listening...")
```

Here we initialize our socket like we did in the beginning of this chapter. We then use the method *bind*, in order to assign the IP-address and the port we chose. Notice that we are passing a tuple as a parameter here. Last but not least, we put our socket to listening mode by using the method *listen*.

After that, we just have to create a loop that accepts the client requests that will eventually come in.

```
                        server.py
import socket

s = socket.socket(socket.AF_INET,
                    socket.SOCK_STREAM)
s.bind(("127.0.0.1", 9999))
s.listen()
print("Listening...")

while True:
    client, address = s.accept()
    print("Connected to
{}".format(address))
    message = "Hello Client!"
    client.send(message.encode('ascii'))
    client.close()
```

The method *accept* waits for a connection attempt to come and accepts it. It then returns a *client* for responses and the *address* of the client that is connected. We can then use this client object in order to send the message. But it's important that we encode the message first, because otherwise we can't send it properly. At the end, we *close* the client because we don't need it anymore.

CREATING A CLIENT

Now our server is done and we just need some clients that connect to it. Our clients shall request a resource from the server. In this case, this is the message *"Hello Client!"*.

For our client we also need a socket but this time it will not use the function *bind* but the function *connect*. So let's start writing our code into a new file.

```python
import socket

s = socket.socket(socket.AF_INET,
                  socket.SOCK_STREAM)
s.connect(("127.0.0.1", 9999))
```

We just create an ordinary internet socket that uses TCP and then connect it to the localhost IP-address at the port 9999.

To now get the message from the server and decode it, we will use the *recv* function.

client.py

```python
import socket

s = socket.socket(socket.AF_INET,
                  socket.SOCK_STREAM)
s.connect(("127.0.0.1", 9999))
message = s.recv(1024)
s.close()
print(message.decode('ascii'))
```

After we connect to the server, we try to receive up to 1024 bytes from it. We then save the message into our variable and then we decode and print it.

CONNECTING SERVER AND CLIENT

Now in order to connect these two entities, we first need to run our server. If there is no server listening on the respective port, our client can't connect to anything. So we run our *server.py* script and start listening.

After that, we can run our *client.py* script many times and they will all connect to the server. The results will look like this:

Server

```
Listening...
Connected to ('127.0.0.1', 4935)
Connected to ('127.0.0.1', 4942)
Connected to ('127.0.0.1', 4943)
Connected to ('127.0.0.1', 4944)
Connected to ('127.0.0.1', 4945)
                  Client
Hello Client!
```

One thing you might optimize on that script if you want is the exception handling. If there is no server listening and our client tries to connect, we get a *ConnectionRefusedError* and our script crashes. Now you can fix this with the knowledge from the first book.

Hint: Use try and except!

PORT SCANNER

Now we have learned a lot about multithreading, locking, queues and sockets. With all that knowledge, we can create a highly efficient and well working *port scanner*.

What a port scanner basically does is: It tries to connect to certain ports at a host or a whole network, in order to find loopholes for future attacks. Open ports mean a security breach. And with our skills, we can already code our own penetration testing tool.

WARNING: *Port scanning is not allowed on any hosts or networks which you don't have explicit permission for. Only scan your own networks or networks for which you were given permission. I don't take any liability for what you do with this knowledge, since I warned you!*

```python
import socket

target = "10.0.0.5"

def portscan(port):
```

```
try:
    s = socket.socket(socket.AF_INET,
                      socket.SOCK_STREAM)
    conn = s.connect((target, port))
    return True
except:
    return False

for x in range(1, 501):
    if(portscan(x)):
        print("Port {} is open!".format(x))
    else:
        print("Port {} is closed!".format(x))
```

So this scanner is quite simple. We define a target address. In this case, this is *10.0.0.5*. Our function *portscan* simply tries to connect to a certain port at that host. If it succeeds, the function returns *True*. If we get an error or an exception, it returns *False*.

This is as simple as a port scan can get. We then use a for loop to scan the first 500 ports and we always print if the port is open or closed.

Just choose a target address and run this script. You will see that it works.

```
Port 21 is closed!
Port 22 is open!
Port 23 is closed!
Port 24 is closed!
Port 25 is open!
```

But you will also notice that it is extremely slow. That's because we serially scan one port after the other. And I think we have already learned how to handle that.

THREADED PORT SCANNER

In order to speed up the scanning process, we are going to use *multithreading*. And to make sure that every port gets scanned and also that no port is scanned twice, we will use *queues.*

```python
import socket
from queue import Queue
import threading

target = "10.0.0.5"

q = Queue()
for x in range(1,501):
    q.put(x)

def portscan(port):
    try:
        s = socket.socket(socket.AF_INET,
                          socket.SOCK_STREAM)
        conn = s.connect((target, port))
        return True
    except:
        return False

def worker():
    while True:
        port = q.get()
        if portscan(port):
            print("Port {} is open!"
                .format(port))
```

So we start by creating a queue and filling it up with all numbers from 1 to 500. We then have two functions. The *portscan* function does the scanning itself and the *worker* function gets all the ports from the queue in order to pass them to the *portscan* function and prints the result. In order to not get confused with the output, we only print when a port is open because we don't care when a port is closed.

Now we just have to decide how many threads we want to start and then we can go for it.

```python
for x in range(30):
    t = threading.Thread(target=worker)
    t.start()
```

In this example, we start 30 threads at the same time. If you run this, you will see that it increases the scanning speed a lot. Within a few seconds, all the 500 ports are scanned. So if you want, you can increase the number to 5000.

The results for my virtual server are the following:

```
Port 25 is open!
Port 22 is open!
Port 80 is open!
Port 110 is open!
Port 119 is open!
Port 143 is open!
Port 443 is open!
Port 465 is open!
```

As you can see, there are a lot of vulnerabilities here. You now just have to google which ports are interesting and depending on your side you may either prepare for an attack or fix the security breaches. For example port 22 is SSH and quite dangerous.

5 – DATABASE PROGRAMMING

Databases are one of the most popular ways to store and manage data in computer science. Because of that, in this chapter we are going to take a look at database programming with Python.

Notice that for most databases we use the query language *SQL*, which stands for *Structured Query Language*. We use this language in order to manage the database, the tables and the rows and columns. This chapter is not about database structure itself, nor is it about SQL. Maybe I will write a specific SQL book in the future but here we are only going to focus on the implementation in Python. We are not going to explain the SQL syntax in too much detail.

CONNECTING TO SQLITE

The database that comes pre-installed with Python is called *SQLite*. It is also the one which we are going to use. Of course, there are also other libraries for *MySQL, MongoDB* etc.

In order to use *SQLite* in Python, we need to import the respective module – *sqlite3*.

```
import sqlite3
```

Now, to create a new database file on our disk, we need to use the *connect* method.

```
conn = sqlite3.connect('mydata.db')
```

This right here creates the new file *mydata.db* and connects to this database. It returns a connection object which we save in the variable *conn*.

EXECUTING STATEMENTS

So, we have established a connection to the database. But in order to execute *SQL* statements, we will need to create a so-called *cursor*.

```
c = conn.cursor()
```

We get this cursor by using the method *cursor* of our connection object that returns it. Now we can go ahead and execute all kinds of statements.

CREATING TABLES

For example, we can create our first table like this:

```
c.execute("""CREATE TABLE persons (
            first_name TEXT,
            last_name TEXT,
            age INTEGER
            )""")
```

Here we use the *execute* function and write our query. What we are passing here is SQL code. As I already said, understanding SQL is not the main objective here. We are focusing on the Python part. Nevertheless, it's quite obvious what's happening here. We are creating a new *table* with the name *persons* and each person will have the three attributes *first_name, last_name* and *age*.

Now our statement is written but in order to really execute it, we ne need to commit to our connection.

```
conn.commit()
```

When we do this, our statement gets executed and our table created. Notice that this works only once, since after that the table already exists and can't be created again.

At the end, don't forget to close the connection, when you are done with everything.

```
conn.close()
```

INSERTING VALUES

Now let's fill up our table with some values. For this, we just use an ordinary *INSERT* statement.

```
c.execute("""INSERT INTO persons VALUES
            ('John', 'Smith', 25),
            ('Anna', 'Smith', 30),
            ('Mike', 'Johnson', 40)""")

conn.commit()
conn.close()
```

So basically, we are just adding three entries to our table. When you run this code, you will see that everything went fine. But to be on the safe side, we will try to now extract the values from the database into our program.

SELECTING VALUES

In order to get values from the database, we need to first execute a *SELECT* statement. After that, we also need to *fetch* the results.

```
c.execute("""SELECT * FROM persons
              WHERE last_name = 'Smith'""")

print(c.fetchall())

conn.commit()
conn.close()
```

As you can see, our *SELECT* statement that gets all the entries where the *last_name* has the value *Smith*. We then need to use the method *fetchall* of the cursor, in order to get our results. It returns a list of tuples, where every tuple is one entry. Alternatively, we could use the method *fetchone* to only get the first entry or *fetchmany* to get a specific amount of entries. In our case however, the result looks like this:

```
[('John', 'Smith', 25), ('Anna', 'Smith', 30)]
```

CLASSES AND TABLES

Now in order to make the communication more efficient and easier, we are going to create a *Person* class that has the columns as attributes.

```python
class Person():

    def __init__(self, first=None,
                     last=None, age=None):
        self.first = first
        self.last = last
        self.age = age

    def clone_person(self, result):
        self.first = result[0]
        self.last = result[1]
        self.age = result[2]
```

Here we have a constructor with default parameters. In case we don't specify any values, they get assigned the value *None*. Also, we have a function *clone_person* that gets passed a sequence and assigns the values of it to the object. In our case, this sequence will be the tuple from the *fetching* results.

FROM TABLE TO OBJECT

So let's create a new *Person* object by getting its data from our database.

```python
c.execute("""SELECT * FROM persons
            WHERE last_name = 'Smith'""")

person1 = Person()
person1.clone_person(c.fetchone())

print(person1.first)
print(person1.last)
print(person1.age)
```

Here we fetch the first entry of our query results, by using the *fetchone* function. The result is the following:

```
John
Smith
25
```

FROM OBJECT TO TABLE

We can also do that the other way around. Let's create a person objects, assign values to the attributes and then insert this object into our database.

```python
person2 = Person("Bob", "Davis", 23)

c.execute("""INSERT INTO persons VALUES
            ('{}', '{}', '{}')"""
        .format(person2.first,
                person2.last,
                person2.age))

conn.commit()
conn.close()
```

Here we used the basic *format* function in order to put our values into the statement. When we execute it, our object gets inserted into the database. We can check this by printing all objects of the table *persons*.

```python
c.execute("SELECT * FROM persons")
print(c.fetchall())
```

In the results, we find our new object:

```
[('John', 'Smith', 25), ('Anna', 'Smith', 30),
('Mike', 'Johnson', 40), ('Bob', 'Davis', 23)]
```

PREPARED STATEMENTS

There is a much more secure and elegant way to put the values of our attributes into the SQL statements. We can use *prepared statements*.

```
person = Person("Julia", "Johnson", 28)

c.execute("INSERT INTO persons VALUES (?, ?,
?)",
          (person.first, person.last,
person.age))

conn.commit()
conn.close()
```

We replace the values with question marks and pass the values as a tuple in the function. This makes our statements cleaner and also less prone to SQL injections.

MORE ABOUT SQL

For this book, we are done with database programming. But there's a lot more to learn about SQL and databases. As I said, I might publish a detailed SQL book in the future so keep checking my author page on Amazon.

However, if you are interested in learning SQL right now, you can check out the W3Schools tutorial.

W3Schools: https://www.w3schools.com/sql/

6 – Recursion

In this short chapter, we are going to talk about a programming concept that I would say should be taught in a book for intermediates. This concept is *recursion* and basically it refers to a function calling itself.

```
def function():
    function()

function()
```

So what do you think happens, when you call a function like that? It is a function that calls itself. And this called function calls itself again and so on. Basically, you get into an endless recursion. This is not very useful and in Python we get an *RecursionError* when the maximum recursion depth is exceeded.

Every program has a stack memory and this memory is limited. When we run a function we allocate stack memory space and if there is no space left, this is called *Stack Overflow*. This is also where the name of the famous forum comes from.

Factorial Calculation

But recursion can also be useful, if it's managed right. For example, we can write a recursive function that calculates the *factorial* of a number. A factorial is just the value you get, when you multiply a number by every lower whole number down to one.

So 10 factorial would be 10 times 9 times 8 and so on until you get to times 1.

```
def factorial(n):
    if n < 1:
        return 1
    else:
        number = n * factorial(n-1)
        return number
```

Look at this function. When we first call it, the parameter *n* is our base number that we want to calculate the factorial of. If *n* is not smaller than one, we multiply it by the factorial of *n-1*. At the end, we return the number.

Notice that our first function call doesn't return anything until we get down to one. This is because it always calls itself in itself over and over again. At the end all the results are multiplied by the last *return* which of course is *one*. Finally, we can print the end result.

This might be quite confusing, if you have never heard of recursion before. Just take your time and analyze what's happening step-by-step here. Try to play around with this concept of *recursion*.

7 – XML Processing

Up until now, we either saved our data into regular text files or into professional databases. Sometimes however, our script is quite small and doesn't need a big database but we still want to structure our data in files. For this, we can use *XML*.

XML stands for *Extensible Markup Language* and is a language that allows us to hierarchically structure our data in files. It is platform-independent and also application-independent. XML files that you create with a Python script, can be read and processed by a C++ or Java application.

XML Parser

In Python, we can choose between two modules for *parsing* XML files – *SAX* and *DOM*.

Simple API for XML (SAX)

SAX stands for *Simple API for XML* and is better suited for large XML files or in situations where we have very limited RAM memory space. This is because in this mode we never load the full file into our RAM. We read the file from our hard drive and only load the little parts that we need right at the moment into the RAM. An additional effect of this is that we can only read from the file and not manipulate it and change values.

DOCUMENT OBJECT MODEL (DOM)

DOM stands for *Document Object Model* and is the generally recommended option. It is a language-independent API for working with XML. Here we always load the full XML file into our RAM and then save it there in a hierarchical structure. Because of that, we can use all of the features and also manipulate the file.

Obviously, DOM is a lot faster than SAX because it is using the RAM instead of the hard disk. The main memory is way more efficient than the hard drive. We only use SAX when our RAM is so limited that we can't even load the full XML file into it without problems.

There is no reason to not use both options in the same projects. We can choose depending on the use case.

XML STRUCTURE

For this chapter, we are going to use the following XML file:

```xml
<?xml version="1.0"?>
<group>
    <person id="1">
        <name>John Smith</name>
        <age>20</age>
        <weight>80</weight>
        <height>188</height>
    </person>
    <person id="2">
        <name>Mike Davis</name>
        <age>45</age>
        <weight>82</weight>
        <height>185</height>
    </person>
    <person id="3">
        <name>Anna Johnson</name>
        <age>33</age>
        <weight>67</weight>
        <height>167</height>
    </person>
    <person id="4">
        <name>Bob Smith</name>
        <age>60</age>
        <weight>70</weight>
        <height>174</height>
    </person>
    <person id="5">
        <name>Sarah Pitt</name>
        <age>12</age>
        <weight>50</weight>
        <height>152</height>
    </person>
</group>
```

As you can see, the structure is quite simple. The first row is just a notation and indicates that we are using XML version one. After that we have various tags. Every tag that gets opened also gets closed at the end.

Basically, we have one *group* tag. Within that, we have multiple *person* tags that all have the attribute *id*. And then again, every *person* has four tags with their values. These tags are the attributes of the respective person. We save this file as *group.xml*.

XML WITH SAX

In order to work with *SAX,* we first need to import the module:

```
import xml.sax
```

Now, what we need in order to process the XML data is a *content handler*. It handles and processes the attributes and tags of the file.

```
import xml.sax

handler = xml.sax.ContentHandler()

parser = xml.sax.make_parser()
parser.setContentHandler(handler)
parser.parse("group.xml")
```

First we create an instance of the *ContentHandler* class. Then we use the method *make_parser,* in order to create a *parser* object. After that, we set our *handler* to the content handler of our parser. We can then parse the file by using the method *parse*.

Now, when we execute our script, we don't see anything. This is because we need to define what happens when an element gets parsed.

CONTENT HANDLER CLASS

For this, we will define our own *content handler* class. Let's start with a very simple example.

```
import xml.sax

class GroupHandler(xml.sax.ContentHandler):
    def startElement(self, name, attrs):
        print(name)

handler = GroupHandler()
parser = xml.sax.make_parser()
parser.setContentHandler(handler)
parser.parse("group.xml")
```

We created a class *GroupHandler* that inherits from *ContentHandler*. Then we overwrite the function *startElement*. Every time an element gets processed, this function gets called. So by manipulating it, we can define what shall happen during the parsing process.

Notice that the function has two parameters – *name* and *attr*. These represent the tag name and the attributes. In our simple example, we just print the tag names. So, let's get to a more interesting example.

PROCESSING XML DATA

The following example is a bit more complex and includes two more functions.

```
import xml.sax

class GroupHandler(xml.sax.ContentHandler):
```

```python
    def startElement(self, name, attrs):
        self.current = name
        if self.current == "person":
            print("--- Person ---")
            id = attrs["id"]
            print("ID: %s" % id)

    def endElement(self, name):
        if self.current == "name":
            print("Name: %s" % self.name)
        elif self.current == "age":
            print("Age: %s" % self.age)
        elif self.current == "weight":
            print("Weight: %s" % self.weight)
        elif self.current == "height":
            print("Height: %s" % self.height)
        self.current = ""

    def characters(self, content):
        if self.current == "name":
            self.name = content
        elif self.current == "age":
            self.age = content
        elif self.current == "weight":
            self.weight = content
        elif self.current == "height":
            self.height = content

handler = GroupHandler()
parser = xml.sax.make_parser()
parser.setContentHandler(handler)
parser.parse("group.xml")
```

The first thing you will notice here is that we have three functions instead of one. When we start processing an element, the function *startElement* gets called. Then we go on to process the individual *characters* which are *name, age, weight* and *height*. At the end of the element parsing, we call the *endElement* function.

In this example, we first check if the element is a *person* or not. If this is the case we print the *id* just for information. We then go on with the *characters* method. It checks which tag belongs to which attribute and saves the values accordingly. At the end, we print out all the values. This is what the results look like:

```
--- Person ---
ID: 1
Name: John Smith
Age: 20
Weight: 80
Height: 188
--- Person ---
ID: 2
Name: Mike Davis
Age: 45
Weight: 82
Height: 185
--- Person ---
...
```

XML WITH DOM

Now, let's look at the DOM option. Here we can not only read from XML files but also change values and attributes. In order to work with DOM, we again need to import the respective module.

```
import xml.dom.minidom
```

When working with DOM, we need to create a so-called *DOM-Tree* and view all elements as collections or sequences.

```
domtree = xml.dom.minidom.parse("group.xml")
group = domtree.documentElement
```

We parse the XML file by using the method *parse*. This returns a DOM-tree, which we save into a variable. Then we get the *documentElement* of our tree and in our case this is *group*. We also save this one into an object.

```
persons = group.getElementsByTagName("person")

for person in persons:
    print("--- Person ---")
    if person.hasAttribute("id"):
        print("ID: %s" %
person.getAttribute("id"))

    name =
person.getElementsByTagName("name")[0]
    age = person.getElementsByTagName("age")[0]
    weight =
person.getElementsByTagName("weight")[0]
    height =
person.getElementsByTagName("height")[0]
```

Now, we can get all the individual elements by using the *getElementsByTagName* function. For example, we save all our *person* tags into a variable by using this method and specifying the name of our desired tags. Our *persons* variable is now a sequence that we can iterate over.

By using the functions *hasAttribute* and *getAttribute,* we can also access the attributes of our tags. In this case, this is only the *id*. In order to get the tag values of the individual person, we again use the method *getElementsByTagName*.

When we do all that and execute our script, we get the exact same result as with *SAX*.

```
--- Person ---
ID: 1
Name: John Smith
Age: 20
Weight: 80
Height: 188
--- Person ---
ID: 2
Name: Mike Davis
Age: 45
Weight: 82
Height: 185
--- Person ---
...
```

MANIPULATING XML FILES

Since we are now working with *DOM*, let's manipulate our XML file and change some values.

```
persons = group.getElementsByTagName("person")

persons[0].getElementsByTagName("name")[0].childNod
es[0].nodeValue = "New Name"
```

As you can see, we are using the same function, to access our elements. Here we adress the *name* tag of the first *person* object. Then we need to access the *childNodes* and change their *nodeValue*. Notice that we only have one element *name* and also only one child node but we still need to address the index zero, for the first element.

In this example, we change the name of the first person to *New Name*. Now in order to apply these changes to the real file, we need to write into it.

```
domtree.writexml(open("group.xml", "w"))
```

We use the *writexml* method of our initial *domtree* object. As a parameter, we pass a file stream that writes into our XML file. After doing that, we can look at the changes.

```
<person id="1">
    <name>New Name</name>
    <age>20</age>
    <weight>80</weight>
    <height>188</height>
</person>
```

We can also change the attributes by using the function *setAttribute*.

```
persons[0].setAttribute("id", "10")
```

Here we change the attribute *id* of the first person to *10*.

```
<person id="10">
    <name>New Name</name>
    <age>20</age>
    <weight>80</weight>
    <height>188</height>
</person>
```

CREATING NEW ELEMENTS

The last thing that we are going to look at in this chapter is creating new XML elements by using DOM. In order to do that, we first need to define a new *person* element.

```
newperson = domtree.createElement("person")
newperson.setAttribute("id", "6")
```

So we use the *domtree* object and the respective method, to create a new XML element. Then we set the *id* attribute to the next number.

After that, we create all the elements that we need for the person and assign values to them.

```
name = domtree.createElement("name")
name.appendChild(domtree.createTextNode("Paul Smith"))

age = domtree.createElement("age")
age.appendChild(domtree.createTextNode("45"))

weight = domtree.createElement("weight")
weight.appendChild(domtree.createTextNode("78"))

height = domtree.createElement("height")
height.appendChild(domtree.createTextNode("178"))
```

First, we create a new element for each attribute of the person. Then we use the method *appendChild* to put something in between the tags of our element. In this case we create a new *TextNode*, which is basically just text.

Last but not least, we again need to use the method *appendChild* in order to define the hierarchical structure. The attribute elements are the childs of the *person* element and this itself is the child of the *group* element.

```
newperson.appendChild(name)
newperson.appendChild(age)
newperson.appendChild(weight)
newperson.appendChild(height)

group.appendChild(newperson)

domtree.writexml(open("group.xml", "w"))
```

When we write these changes into our file, we can see the following results:

```
<person id="6">
    <name>Paul Smith</name>
    <age>45</age>
    <weight>78</weight>
    <height>178</height>
</person>
```

8 – Logging

No matter what we do in computer science, sooner or later we will need logs. Every system that has a certain size produces errors or conditions in which specific people should be warned or informed. Nowadays, everything gets logged or recorded. Bank transactions, flights, networking activities, operating systems and much more. Log files help us to find problems and to get information about the state of our systems. They are an essential tool for avoiding and understanding errors.

Up until now, we have always printed some message onto the console screen when we encountered an error. But when our applications grow, this becomes confusing and we need to categorize and outsource our logs. In addition, not every message is equally relevant. Some messages are urgent because a critical component fails and some just provide nice information.

Security Levels

In Python, we have got five security levels. A higher level means higher importance or urgency.

1. DEBUG
2. INFO
3. WARNING
4. ERROR
5. CRITICAL

Notice that when we choose a certain security level, we also get all the messages of the levels above. So for example, *INFO* also prints the messages of *WARNING, ERROR* and *CRITICAL* but not of *DEBUG*.

DEBUG is mainly used for tests, experiments or in order to check something. We typically use this mode, when we are looking for errors (troubleshooting).

We use *INFO* when we want to log all the important events that inform us about what is happening. This might be something like *"User A logged in successfully!"* or *"Now we have 17 users online!"*

WARNING messages are messages that inform us about irregularities and things that might go wrong and become a problem. For example messages like *"Only 247 MB of RAM left!"*

An *ERROR* message gets logged or printed when something didn't go according to the plan. When we get an exception this is a classical error.

CRITICAL messages tell us that critical for the whole system or application happened. This might be the case when a crucial component fails and we have to immediately stop all operations.

CREATING LOGGERS

In order to create a logger in Python, we need to import the *logging* module.

```
import logging
```

Now we can just log messages by directly using the respective functions of the *logging* module.

```
logging.info("First informational
message!")
logging.critical("This is serious!")
```

This works because we are using the *root* logger. We haven't created our own loggers yet. The output looks like this:

```
CRITICAL:root:This is serious!
INFO:root:Logger successfully created!
```

So let's create our own logger now. This is done by either using the constructor of the *Logger* class or by using the method *getLogger*.

```
logger = logging.getLogger()
logger = logging.Logger("MYLOGGER")
```

Notice that we need to specify a name for our logger, if we use the constructor. Now we can log our messages.

```
logger.info("Logger successfully created!")
logger.log(logging.INFO, "Successful!")
logger.critical("Critical Message!")
logger.log(logging.CRITICAL, "Critical!")
```

Here we also have two different options for logging messages. We can either directly call the function of the respective security level or we can use the method *log* and specify the security level in the parameters.

But when you now execute the script, you will notice that it will only print the critical messages. This has two reasons. First of all, we need to adjust the level of the logger and second of all, we need to remove all of the *handlers* from the default *root* logger.

```
for handler in logging.root.handlers:
    logging.root.removeHandler(handler)
logging.basicConfig(level=logging.INFO)
```

Here we just use a for loop in order to remove all the handlers from the root logger. Then we use the *basicConfig* method, in order to set our logging level to *INFO*. When we now run our code again, the output is the following:

```
INFO:MYLOGGER:Logger successfully created!
INFO:MYLOGGER:Successful!
CRITICAL:MYLOGGER:Critical Message!
CRITICAL:MYLOGGER:Critical!
```

LOGGING INTO FILES

What we are mainly interested in is logging into files. For this, we need a so-called *FileHandler*. It is an object that we add to our logger, in order to make it log everything into a specific file.

```
import logging

logger = logging.getLogger("MYLOGGER")
logger.setLevel(logging.INFO)

handler =
logging.FileHandler("logfile.log")
handler.setLevel(logging.INFO)

logger.addHandler(handler)
logger.info("Log this into the file!")
logger.critical("This is critical!")
```

We start again by defining a logger. Then we set the security level to *INFO* by using the function *setLevel*. After that, we create a *FileHandler* that logs into the file *logfile.log*. Here we also need to set the security level. Finally, we add the handler to our logger using the *addHandler* function and start logging messages.

FORMATTING LOGS

One thing that you will notice is that we don't have any format in our logs. We don't know which logger was used or which security level our message has. For this, we can use a so-called *formatter*.

```python
import logging

logger = logging.getLogger()
logger.setLevel(logging.INFO)

handler =
logging.FileHandler("logfile.log")
handler.setLevel(logging.INFO)

formatter = logging.Formatter('%(asctime)s:
%(levelname)s - %(message)s')
handler.setFormatter(formatter)

logger.addHandler(handler)
logger.info("This will get into the file!")
```

We create a formatter by using the constructor of the respective class. Then we use the keywords for the timestamp, the security level name and the message. Last but not least, we assign the formatter to our handler and start logging again. When we now look into our file, we will find a more detailed message.

```
2019-06-25 15:41:43,523: INFO - This will get into the
file!
```

These log messages can be very helpful, if they are used wisely. Place them wherever something important or alarming happens in your code.

9 – REGULAR EXPRESSIONS

In programming, you will oftentimes have to deal with long texts from which we want to extract specific information. Also, when we want to process certain inputs, we need to check for a specific pattern. For example, think about emails. They need to have some text, followed by an @ character, then again some text and finally a *dot* and again some little text.

In order to make the validations easier, more efficient and more compact, we use so-called *regular expressions*.

The topic of regular expressions is very huge and you could write a whole book only about it. This is why we are not going to focus too much on the various placeholders and patterns of the expressions themselves but on the implementation of *RegEx* in Python.

So in order to confuse you right in the beginning, let's look at a regular expression that checks if the format of an email-address is valid.

```
^[a-zA-Z0-9.!#$%&'*+/=?^_`{|}~-]+@[a-zA-Z0-
9](?:[a-zA-Z0-9-]{0,61}[a-zA-Z0-9])?(?:\.[a-zA-
Z0-9](?:[a-zA-Z0-9-]{0,61}[a-zA-Z0-9])?)*$
```

Now you can see why this is a huge field to learn. In this chapter, we are not going to build regular expressions like this. We are going to focus on quite simple examples and how to properly implement them in Python.

IDENTIFIER

Let's get started with some basic knowledge first. So-called *identifiers* define what kind of character should be at a certain place. Here you have some examples:

REGEX IDENTIFIERS	
IDENTIFIER	**DESCRIPTION**
\d	Some digit
\D	Everything BUT a digit
\s	White space
\S	Everything BUT a white space
\w	Some letter
\W	Everything BUT a letter
.	Every character except for new lines
\b	White spaces around a word
\.	A dot

MODIFIER

The *modifiers* extend the regular expressions and the identifiers. They might be seen as some kind of operator for regular expressions.

REGEX MODIFIERS

MODIFIER	DESCRIPTION
{x,y}	A number that has a length between x and y
+	At least one
?	None or one
*	Everything
$	At the end of a string
^	At the beginning of a string
|	Either Or Example: x | y = either x or y
[]	Value range
{x}	x times
{x,y}	x to y times

ESCAPE CHARACTERS

Last but not least, we have the classic *escape characters.*

REGEX ESCAPE CHARATCERS	
CHARACTER	**DESCRIPTION**
\n	New Line
\t	Tab
\s	White Space

Applying Regular Expressions

Finding Strings

In order to apply these regular expressions in Python, we need to import the module *re*.

```
import re
```

Now we can start by trying to find some patterns in our strings.

```
text = '''
Mike is 20 years old and George is 29!
My grandma is even 104 years old!
'''

ages = re.findall(r'\d{1,3}', text)
print(ages)
```

In this example, we have a text with three ages in it. What we want to do is to filter these out and print them separately.

As you can see, we use the function *findall* in order to apply the regular expression onto our string. In this case, we are looking for numbers that are one to three digits long. Notice that we are using an *r* character before we write our expression. This indicates that the given string is a regular expression.

At the end, we print our result and get the following output:

```
['20', '29', '104']
```

MATCHING STRINGS

What we can also do is to check if a string matches a certain regular expression. For example, we can apply our regular expression for mails here.

```
import re

text = "test@mail.com"

result = re.fullmatch(r"^[a-zA-Z0-
9.!#$%&'*+/=?^_`{|}~-]+@[a-zA-Z0-9](?:[a-
zA-Z0-9-]{0,61}[a-zA-Z0-9])?(?:\.[a-zA-Z0-
9](?:[a-zA-Z0-9-]{0,61}[a-zA-Z0-9])?)*$",
text)

if result != None:
    print("VALID!")
else:
    print("INVALID!")
```

We are not going to talk about the regular expression itself here. It is very long and complicated. But what we see here is a new function called *fullmatch*. This function returns the checked string if it matches the regular expression. In this case, this happens when the string has a valid mail format.

If the expression doesn't match the string, the function returns *None*. In our example above, we get the message *"VALID!"* since the expression is met. If we enter something like *"Hello World!"*, we will get the other message.

MANIPULATING STRINGS

Finally, we are going to take a look at manipulating strings with regular expressions. By using the function *sub* we can replace all the parts of a string that match the expression by something else.

```
import re

text = """
Mike is 20 years old and George is 29!
My grandma is even 104 years old!
"""

text = re.sub(r'\d{1,3}', "100", text)
print(text)
```

In this example, we replace all ages by *100*. This is what gets printed:

```
Mike is 100 years old and George is 100!
My grandma is even 100 years old!
```

These are the basic functions that we can operate with in Python when dealing with regular expressions. If you want to learn more about regular expressions just google and you will find a lot of guides. Play around with the identifiers and modifiers a little bit until you feel like you understand how they work.

WHAT'S NEXT?

Now you have finished reading the second volume of this Python Bible series. This one was way more complex than the first one and it had a lot more content. Make sure that you practice what you've learned. If necessary, reread this book a couple of times and play around with the code samples. That will dramatically increase the value that you can get out of this book.

However, you are now definitely able to develop some advanced and professional Python applications. You can develop a chat, a port scanner, a string formatter and many more ideas. But this is still just the beginning. Even though you can now consider yourself to be an advanced Python programmer, there is much more to learn.

With the next volumes we are going to dive deep into the fields of machine learning, data science and finance. By having read the first two volumes you already have an excellent basis and I encourage you to continue your journey. I hope you could get some value out of this book and that it helped you to become a better programmer. So stay tuned and prepare for the next volume!

Last but not least, a little reminder. This book was written for you, so that you can get as much value as possible and learn to code effectively. If you find this book valuable or you think you learned something new, please write a quick review on Amazon. It is completely free and takes about one minute. But it helps me produce more high quality books, which you can benefit from.

Thank you!

3

PYTHON BIBLE

DATA SCIENCE

FLORIAN DEDOV

THE PYTHON BIBLE

VOLUME THREE
DATA SCIENCE

BY

FLORIAN DEDOV

Copyright © 2019

TABLE OF CONTENT

INTRODUCTION

In our modern time, the amount of data grows exponentially. Over time, we learn to extract important information out of this data by analyzing it. The field which is primarily focusing on exactly that is called *data science*. We use data science to analyze share prices, the weather, demographics or to create powerful artificial intelligences. Every modern and big system has to deal with tremendous amounts of data that need to be managed and analyzed intelligently.

Therefore, it is more than reasonable to educate yourself in this area as much as possible. Otherwise you might get overrun by this fast-growing trend instead of being part of it.

THIS BOOK

If you have read the first two volumes of this series, you are already a decent Python programmer. You are able to develop complex scripts using advanced techniques like multithreading or network programming. A lot of these skills will be needed for this volume, since it's going to be quite complex and detailed.

Now in this volume, we are going to start by talking about the major libraries or modules for data science in Python. We are taking a look at advanced arrays and lists, professional data visualization, statistical analysis and advanced data science with data frames. At the end, you will be able to prepare, analyze and visualize your own big data sets. This will lay the foundations for future volumes about machine learning and finance.

This book is again full of new and more complex information. There is a lot to learn here so stay tuned and code along while reading. This will help you to understand the material better and to practice implementing it. I wish you a lot of fun and success with your journey and this book!

Just one little thing before we start. This book was written for you, so that you can get as much value as possible and learn to code effectively. If you find this book valuable or you think you have learned something new, please write a quick review on Amazon. It is completely free and takes about one minute. But it helps me produce more high quality books, which you can benefit from.

Thank you!

1 – WHAT IS DATA SCIENCE?

Now before we do anything at all, we need to first define what we are even talking about when using the term *data science*. What is data science?

When we are dealing with data science or data analysis, we are always trying to generate or extract knowledge from our data. For this, we use models, techniques and theories from the areas of mathematics, statistics, computer science, machine learning and many more.

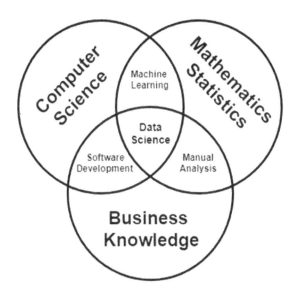

The figure above illustrates pretty accurately what data science actually is. When you combine computer science and business knowledge, you get software development and create business applications. When you combine your business knowledge with mathematics and statistics, you can also analyze the data but you have to do it manually, since you are missing the computational component. When you only combine computer science and statistics, you get machine learning, which is very powerful, but without the necessary business knowledge, you won't get any significant information or conclusions. We need to combine all of these three areas, in order to end up with data science.

However, in this volume we are not going to focus too much on the mathematics and the statistics or the machine learning algorithms. This will be the topic of future volumes. In this book we are focusing on the structuring, visualization and analyzing of the data.

WHY PYTHON?

Now, you should already know why Python is a good choice and a good programming language to learn. But why should we use it for data science? Aren't there better alternatives?

And although I hate polarizing answers and generalization, I have to bluntly say **NO!** You have some alternatives like the programming language *R* or *MATLAB* but they are not as big, as powerful and as simple as Python.

One of the main reasons for Python's popularity in this area is the large amount of libraries and modules for data science but also machine learning and scientific computing. We already have professional open-source libraries for managing lists, linear algebra, data visualization, machine learning, neural networks and much more.

Also, alternatives like R or MATLAB are very specialized in one single area like statistics or mathematical programming. Python on the other hand is a general-purpose language. We use it to code network scripts, video games, professional web applications, artificial intelligences and much more. Self-driving cars use Python, professional modelling software uses Python and also Pinterest was developed with Django, which is a Python framework.

For these reasons, Python has become one of the most popular programming languages out there, especially for machine learning and data science.

2 – INSTALLING MODULES

So the last thing we need to talk about before we get into the coding itself is the modules or libraries that we are going to use.

The following figure illustrates the structure of the modules that are used for data science and scientific computing.

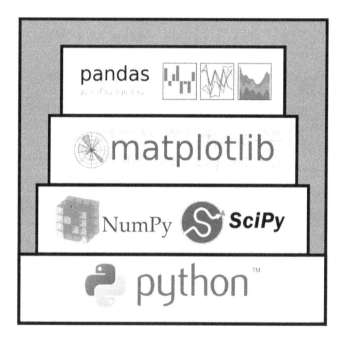

As you can see, we have four major modules here and they all build on core Python. Basically, this is the hierarchy of these modules. *NumPy* builds on Python, *Matplotlib* uses or builds on *NumPy* and

Pandas builds on top of that. Of course there are other libraries that then build on top of *Pandas* as well. But for now, these are the modules that interest us.

Now in order to clear up the confusion, let's look at the purpose and functionalities of the individual libraries.

NUMPY

The *NumPy* module allows us to efficiently work with vectors, matrices and multi-dimensional arrays. It is crucial for linear algebra and numerical analysis. Also, it offers some advanced things like Fourier transforms and random number generation. It basically replaces the primitive and inefficient Python *list* with very powerful *NumPy arrays*.

Another thing worth mentioning is that NumPy was built in the *C* programming language. This means that it is a lot faster and more efficient than other Python libraries.

SCIPY

SciPy is a module which we are actually not going to use in this book. Nevertheless, it is worth mentioning because it is a very powerful library for scientific computing (maybe there will be a future volume about this).

However, SciPy can be seen as the application of NumPy to real problems. NumPy is basically just managing the arrays and lists. It is responsible for the operations like indexing, sorting, slicing, reshaping and so on. Now, SciPy actually uses NumPy to offer more abstract classes and functions that solve scientific problems. It gets deeper into the mathematics and adds substantial capabilities to NumPy.

MATPLOTLIB

On top of that, we have *Matplotlib*. This library is responsible for plotting graphs and visualizing our data. It offers numerous types of plotting, styles and graphs.

Visualization is a key step in data science. When we see our data in form of a graph, we can extract information and spot relations much easier. With Matplotlib we can do this professionally and very easy.

PANDAS

Last but not least, we have *Pandas*. This is the most high-level of our libraries and it builds on top of them. It offers us a powerful data structure named *data frame*. You can imagine it to be a bit like a mix of an Excel table and an SQL database table.

This library allows us to efficiently work with our huge amounts of interrelated data. We can merge, reshape, filter and query our data. We can iterate over it and we can read and write into files like CSV, XLSX and more. Also, it is very powerful when we work with databases, due to the similar structure of the tables.

Pandas is highly compatible with NumPy and Matplotlib, since it builds on them. We can easily convert data from one format to the other.

INSTALLING MODULES WITH PIP

Since all these modules don't belong to core Python, we will need to install them externally. For this, we are going to use *pip*. This is a recursive name and stands for *pip installs packages*.

In order to use pip, we just need to open up our terminal or command line. On windows this is CMD and on Mac and Linux it is the terminal. We then just use the following syntax, in order to install the individual packages.

```
pip install <package-name>
```

So what we need to do is to execute the following commands:

```
pip install numpy
```

```
pip install scipy (optional)
```

```
pip install matplotlib
```

```
pip install pandas
```

3 – NUMPY ARRAYS

We can't do a lot of data science with NumPy alone. But it provides the basis for all the high-level libraries or modules for data science. It is essential for the efficient management of arrays and linear algebra.

In order to use NumPy, we of course have to import the respective module first.

```
import numpy as np
```

As you can see, we are also defining an *alias* here, so that we can address NumPy by just writing *np*.

CREATING ARRAYS

To create a NumPy array, we just use the respective function *array* and pass a list to it.

```
a = np.array([10, 20, 30])
b = np.array([1, 77, 2, 3])
```

Now we can access the values in the same way as we would do it with a list.

```
print(a[0])
print(b[2])
```

MULTI-DIMENSIONAL ARRAYS

The arrays we created are one-dimensional arrays. With NumPy, we can create large multi-dimensional arrays that have the same structure as a matrix.

```
a = np.array([
    [10, 20, 30],
    [40, 50, 60]
])
```

```
print(a)
```

Here, we pass two lists within a list as a parameter. This creates a 2x3 matrix. When we print the array, we get the following result:

```
[[10 20 30]
 [40 50 60]]
```

Since we now have two dimensions, we also need to address two indices, in order to access a specific element.

```
print(a[1][2])
```

In this case, we are addressing the second row (index one) and the third element or column (index two). Therefore, our result is *60*.

We can extend this principle as much as we want. For example, let's create a much bigger array.

```
a = np.array([
    [
        [10,20,30,40], [8,8,2,1], [1,1,1,2]
    ],
    [
        [9, 9, 2, 39], [1,2,3,3], [0,0,3,2]
    ],
    [
        [12,33,22,1], [22,1,22,2],
[0,2,3,1]
    ]
], dtype=float)
```

Here we have a 3x3x4 matrix and slowly but surely it becomes a bit irritating and we can't really grasp the structure of the array. This is especially the case when we get into four or more dimensions, since we only perceive three dimensions in everyday life.

You can imagine this three-dimensional array as a cube. We have three rows, four columns and three pages or layers. Such visualizations fail in higher dimensions.

Another thing that is worth mentioning is the parameter *dtype*. It stands for data type and allows us to specify which data type our values have. In this case we specified *float* and therefore our values will be stored as floating point numbers with the respective notation.

FILLING ARRAYS

Instead of manually filling our arrays with values, we can also use pre-defined functions in certain cases. The only thing we need to specify is the desired function and the shape of the array.

FULL FUNCTION

By using the *full* function for example, we fill an array of a certain shape with the same number. In this case we create a 3x5x4 matrix, which is filled with sevens.

```
a = np.full((3,5,4), 7)

print(a)
```

When we print it, we get the following output:

```
[[[7 7 7 7]
  [7 7 7 7]
  [7 7 7 7]]

 [[7 7 7 7]
  [7 7 7 7]
  [7 7 7 7]]]
```

ZEROS AND ONES

For the cases that we want arrays full of zeros or ones, we even have specific functions.

```
a = np.zeros((3,3))
b = np.ones((2,3,4,2))
```

Here we create a 3x3 array full of zeros and a four-dimensional array full of ones.

EMPTY AND RANDOM

Other options would be to create an empty array or one that is filled with random numbers. For this, we use the respective functions once again.

```
a = np.empty((4,4))
b = np.random.random((2,3))
```

The function *empty* creates an array without initializing the values at all. This makes it a little bit faster but also more dangerous to use, since the user needs to manually initialize all the values.

When using the *random* function, make sure that you are referring to the module *np.random*. You need to write it two times because otherwise you are calling the library.

RANGES

Instead of just filling arrays with the same values, we can fill create sequences of values by specifying the boundaries. For this, we can use two different functions, namely *arange and linspace*.

```
a = np.arange(10, 50, 5)
```

The function *arange* creates a list with values that range from the minimum to the maximum. The step-size has to be specified in the parameters.

```
[10 15 20 25 30 35 40 45]
```

In this example, we create have count from 10 to 45 by always adding 5. The result can be seen above.

By using *linspace* we also create a list from a minimum value to a maximum value. But instead of specifying the step-size, we specify the amount of values that we want to have in our list. They will all be spread evenly and have the same distance to their neighbors.

```
b = np.linspace(0, 100, 11)
```

Here, we want to create a list that ranges from 0 to 100 and contains 11 elements. This fits smoothly with a difference of 10 between all numbers. So the result looks like this:

```
[  0.   10.   20.   30.   40.   50.   60.   70.   80.   90.
100.]
```

Of course, if we choose different parameters, the numbers don't be that "beautiful".

NOT A NUMBER (NAN)

There is a special value in NumPy that represents values that are not numbers. It is called *NaN* and stands for *Not a Number*. We basically just use it as a placeholder for empty spaces. It can be seen as a value that indicates that something is missing at that place.

When importing big data packets into our application, there will sometimes be missing data. Instead of just setting these values to zero or something else, we can set them to NaN and then filter these data sets out.

ATTRIBUTES OF ARRAYS

NumPy arrays have certain attributes that we can access and that provide information about the structure of it.

NUMPY ARRAY ATTRIBUTES	
ATTRIBUTE	**DESCRIPTION**
a.shape	Returns the shape of the array e.g. (3,3) or (3,4,7)
a.ndim	Returns how many dimensions our array has
a.size	Returns the amount of elements an array has
a.dtype	Returns the data type of the values in the array

MATHEMATICAL OPERATIONS

Now that we know how to create an array and what attributes it has, let's take a look at how to work with arrays. For this, we will start out with basic mathematical operations.

ARITHMETIC OPERATIONS

```
a = np.array([
    [1,4,2],
    [8,8,2]
])

print(a + 2)
print(a - 2)
print(a * 2)
print(a / 2)
```

When we perform basic arithmetic operations like addition, subtraction, multiplication and division to an array and a scalar, we apply the operation on every single element in the array. Let's take a look at the results:

```
[[ 3  6  4]
 [10 10  4]]
[[-1  2  0]
 [ 6  6  0]]
[[ 2  8  4]
 [16 16  4]]
[[0.5 2.  1. ]
 [4.  4.  1. ]]
```

As you can see, when we multiply the array by two, we multiply every single value in it by two. This is also the case for addition, subtraction and division. But what happens when we apply these operations on two arrays?

```
a = np.array([
    [1,4,2],
    [8,8,2]
])

b = np.array([
    [1,2,3]
])

c = np.array([
    [1],
    [2]
])

d = np.array([
    [1,2,3],
    [3,2,1]
])
```

In order to apply these operations on two arrays, we need to take care of the shapes. They don't have to be the same, but there has to be a reasonable way of performing the operations. We then again apply the operations on each element of the array.

For example, look at *a* and *b*. They have different shapes but when we add these two, they share at least the amount of columns.

```
print(a+b)
```

```
[[ 2  6  5]
 [ 9 10  5]]
```

Since they match the columns, we can just say that we add the individual columns, even if the amount of rows differs.

The same can also be done with *a* and *c* where the rows match and the columns differ.

```
print(a+c)
```

```
[[ 2  5  3]
 [10 10  4]]
```

And of course it also works, when the shapes match exactly. The only problem is when the shapes differ too much and there is no reasonable way of performing the operations. In these cases, we get *ValueErrors*.

MATHEMATICAL FUNCTIONS

Another thing that the NumPy module offers us is mathematical functions that we can apply to each value in an array.

NUMPY MATHEMATICAL FUNCTIONS	
FUNCTION	DESCRIPTION
np.exp(a)	Takes *e* to the power of each value
np.sin(a)	Returns the sine of each value
np.cos(a)	Returns the cosine of each value
np.tan(a)	Returns the tangent of each value
np.log(a)	Returns the logarithm of each value
np.sqrt(a)	Returns the square root of each value

AGGREGATE FUNCTIONS

Now we are getting into the statistics. NumPy offers us some so-called *aggregate functions* that we can use in order to get a key statistic from all of our values.

NUMPY AGGREGATE FUNCTIONS	
FUNCTION	**DESCRIPTION**
a.sum()	Returns the sum of all values in the array
a.min()	Returns the lowest value of the array
a.max()	Returns the highest value of the array
a.mean()	Returns the arithmetic mean of all values in the array
np.median(a)	Returns the median value of the array
np.std(a)	Returns the standard deviation of the values in the array

MANIPULATING ARRAYS

NumPy offers us numerous ways in which we can manipulate the data of our arrays. Here, we are going to take a quick look at the most important functions and categories of functions.

If you just want to change a single value however, you can just use the basic indexing of lists.

```
a = np.array([
    [4, 2, 9],
    [8, 3, 2]
])

a[1][2] = 7
```

SHAPE MANIPULATION FUNCTIONS

One of the most important and helpful types of functions are the *shape manipulating functions*. These allow us to restructure our arrays without changing their values.

SHAPE MANIPULATION FUNCTIONS	
FUNCTION	**DESCRIPTION**
a.reshape(x,y)	Returns an array with the same values structured in a different shape
a.flatten()	Returns a flattened one-dimensional copy of the array
a.ravel()	Does the same as *flatten* but works with the actual array instead of a copy
a.transpose()	Returns an array with the same values but swapped dimensions
a.swapaxes()	Returns an array with the same values but two swapped axes
a.flat	Not a function but an iterator for the flattened version of the array

There is one more element that is related to shape but it's not a function. It is called *flat* and it is an iterator for the flattened one-dimensional version of the array. *Flat* is not callable but we can iterate over it with *for* loops or index it.

```
for x in a.flat:
    print(x)

print(a.flat[5])
```

JOINING FUNCTIONS

We use *joining functions* when we combine multiple arrays into one new array.

JOINING FUNCTIONS	
FUNCTION	**DESCRIPTION**
np.concatenate(a,b)	Joins multiple arrays along an existing axis
np.stack(a,b)	Joins multiple arrays along a new axis
np.hstack(a,b)	Stacks the arrays horizontally (column-wise)
np.vstack(a,b)	Stacks the arrays vertically (row-wise)

In the following, you can see the difference between *concatenate* and *stack*:

```
a = np.array([10, 20, 30])
b = np.array([20, 20, 10])

print(np.concatenate((a,b)))
print(np.stack((a,b)))
```

```
[10 20 30 20 20 10]
[[10 20 30]
 [20 20 10]]
```

What *concatenate* does is, it joins the arrays together by just appending one onto the other. *Stack* on the other hand, creates an additional axis that separates the two initial arrays.

SPLITTING FUNCTIONS

We can not only join and combine arrays but also split them again. This is done by using *splitting functions* that split arrays into multiple sub-arrays.

SPLITTING FUNCTIONS	
FUNCTION	**DESCRIPTION**
np.split(a, x)	Splits one array into multiple arrays
np.hsplit(a, x)	Splits one array into multiple arrays horizontally (column-wise)
np.vsplit(a, x)	Splits one array into multiple arrays vertically (row-wise)

When splitting a list with the *split* function, we need to specify into how many sections we want to split our array.

```
a = np.array([
    [10, 20, 30],
    [40, 50, 60],
    [70, 80, 90],
    [100, 110, 120]
])

print(np.split(a, 2))
print(np.split(a, 4))
```

This array can be split into either two or four equally sized arrays on the default axis. The two possibilities are the following:

```
1: [[10, 20, 30],[40, 50, 60]]
2: [[70, 80, 90],[100, 110, 120]]
```

OR

```
1: [[10, 20, 30]]
2: [[40, 50, 60]]
3: [[70, 80, 90]]
4: [[100, 110, 120]]
```

ADDING AND REMOVING

The last manipulating functions that we are going to look at are the ones which allow us to *add* and to *remove* items.

ADDING AND REMOVING FUNCTIONS	
FUNCTION	**DESCRIPTION**
np.resize(a, (x,y))	Returns a resized version of the array and fills empty spaces by repeating copies of a
np.append(a, [...])	Appends values at the end of the array
np.insert(a, x, ...)	Insert a value at the index x of the array
np.delete(a, x, y)	Delete axes of the array

LOADING AND SAVING ARRAYS

Now last but not least, we are going to talk about loading and saving NumPy arrays. For this, we can use the integrated NumPy format or CSV-files.

NUMPY FORMAT

Basically, we are just serializing the object so that we can use it later. This is done by using the *save* function.

```
a = np.array([
    [10, 20, 30],
    [40, 50, 60],
    [70, 80, 90],
    [100, 110, 120]
])

np.save('myarray.npy', a)
```

Notice that you don't have to use the file ending *npy*. In this example, we just use it for clarity. You can pick whatever you want.

Now, in order to load the array into our script again, we will need the *load* function.

```
a = np.load('myarray.npy')
print(a)
```

CSV FORMAT

As I already mentioned, we can also save our NumPy arrays into CSV files, which are just comma-separated text files. For this, we use the function *savetxt*.

```
np.savetxt('myarray.csv', a)
```

Our array is now stored in a CSV-file which is very useful, because it can then also be read by other applications and scripts.

In order to read this CSV-file back into our script, we use the function *loadtxt*.

```
a = np.loadtxt('myarray.csv')
print(a)
```

If we want to read in a CSV-file that uses another separator than the default one, we can specify a certain delimiter.

```
a = np.loadtxt('myarray.csv',
delimiter=';')
print(a)
```

Now it uses semi-colons as separator when reading
the file. The same can also be done with the saving
or writing function.

4 – MATPLOTLIB DIAGRAMS

We have already mentioned that visualizing our data is crucial for data science. It gives us an overview and helps us to analyze data and make conclusions. Therefore, we will talk quite a lot about *Matplotlib*, the library which we use for plotting and visualizing.

PLOTTING MATHEMATICAL FUNCTIONS

Now, let's start out by drawing some mathematical functions first. In order to do so, we need to import the *matplotlib.pyplot* module and also NumPy.

```
import numpy as np
import matplotlib.pyplot as plt
```

Notice that we are also using an alias for *pyplot* here. In this case, it is *plt*.

In order to plot a function, we need the x-values or the input and the y-values or the output. So let us generate our x-values first.

```
x_values = np.linspace(0, 20, 100)
```

We are doing this by using the already known *linspace* function. Here we create an array with 100 values between 0 and 20. To now get our y-values, we just need to apply the respective function on our x-values. For this example, we are going with the sine function.

```
y_values = np.sin(x_values)
```

Remember that the function gets applied to every single item of the input array. So in this case, we have an array with the sine value of every element of the x-values array. We just need to plot them now.

```
plt.plot(x_values, y_values)
plt.show()
```

We do this by using the function *plot* and passing our x-values and y-values. At the end we call the *show* function, to display our plot.

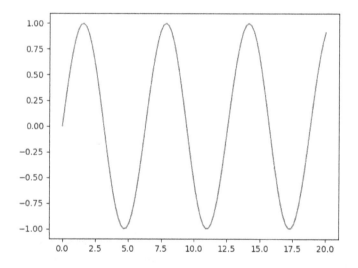

That was very simple. Now, we can go ahead and define our own function that we want to plot.

```
x = np.linspace(0, 10, 100)
y = (6 * x - 30) ** 2

plt.plot(x, y)
plt.show()
```

The result looks like this:

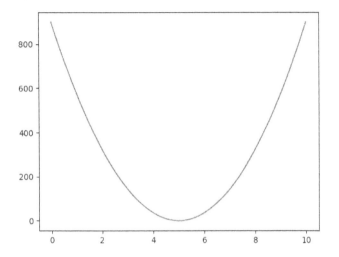

This is just the function $(6x - 30)^2$ plotted with Matplotlib.

VISUALIZING VALUES

What we can also do, instead of plotting functions, is just visualizing values in form of single dots for example.

```
numbers = 10 * np.random.random(100)

plt.plot(numbers, 'bo')
plt.show()
```

Here we are just generating 100 random numbers from 0 to 10. We then plot these numbers as blue dots. This is defined by the second parameter *'bo'*, where the first letter indicates the color (blue) and the second one the shape (dots). Here you can see what this looks like:

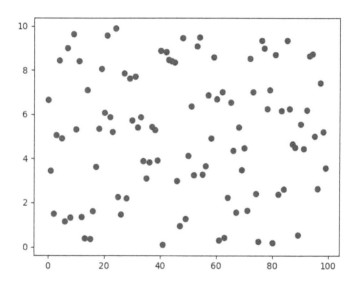

MULTIPLE GRAPHS

Our plots are not limited to only one single graph. We can plot multiple functions in different color and shape.

```
x = np.linspace(0,5,200)
y1 = 2 * x
y2 = x ** 2
y3 = np.log(x)

plt.plot(x, y1)
plt.plot(x, y2)
plt.plot(x, y3)
plt.show()
```

In this example, we first generate 200 x-values from 0 to 5. Then we define three different functions *y1, y2* and *y3*. We plot all these and view the plotting window. This is what it looks like:

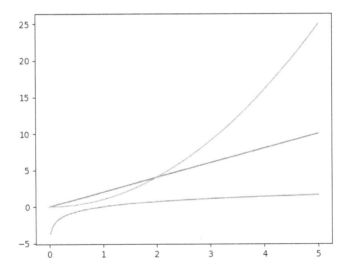

SUBPLOTS

Now, sometimes we want to draw multiple graphs but we don't want them in the same plot necessarily. For this reason, we have so-called *subplots*. These are plots that are shown in the same window but independently from each other.

```
x = np.linspace(0,5,200)
y1 = np.sin(x)
y2 = np.sqrt(x)

plt.subplot(211)
plt.plot(x, y1, 'r-')

plt.subplot(212)
plt.plot(x, y2, 'g--')

plt.show()
```

By using the function *subplot* we state that everything we plot now belongs to this specific subplot. The parameter we pass defines the grid of our window. The first digit indicates the number of rows, the second the number of columns and the last one the index of the subplot. So in this case, we have two rows and one column. Index one means that the respective subplot will be at the top.

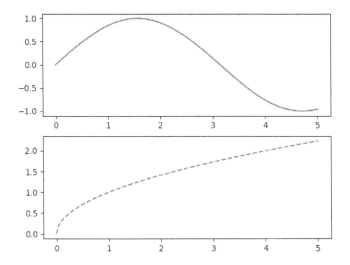

As you can see, we have two subplots in one window and both have a different color and shape. Notice that the ratios between the x-axis and the y-axis differ in the two plots.

MULTIPLE PLOTTING WINDOWS

Instead of plotting into subplots, we can also go ahead and plot our graphs into multiple windows. In Matplotlib we call these *figures*.

```
plt.figure(1)
plt.plot(x, y1, 'r-')

plt.figure(2)
plt.plot(x, y2, 'g--')
```

By doing this, we can show two windows with their graphs at the same time. Also, we can use subplots within figures.

PLOTTING STYLES

Matplotlib offers us many different plotting styles to choose from. If you are interested in how they look when they are applied, you can see an overview by going to the following website (I used a URL shortener to make it more readable):

https://bit.ly/2JfhJ4o

In order to use a style, we need to import the *style* module of Matplotlib and then call the function *use*.

```
from matplotlib import style

style.use('ggplot')
```

By using the *from ... import ...* notation we don't need to specify the parent module *matplotlib*. Here we apply the style of *ggplot*. This adds a grid and some other design changes to our plots. For more information, check out the link above.

LABELING DIAGRAMS

In order to make our graphs understandable, we need to label them properly. We should label the axes, we should give our windows titles and in some cases we should also add a legend.

SETTING TITLES

Let's start out by setting the titles of our graphs and windows.

```
x = np.linspace(0,50,100)
y = np.sin(x)

plt.title("Sine Function")
plt.suptitle("Data Science")
plt.grid(True)
plt.plot(x,y)

plt.show()
```

In this example, we used the two functions *title* and *suptitle*. The first function adds a simple title to our plot and the second one adds an additional centered title above it. Also, we used the *grid* function, to turn on the grid of our plot.

If you want to change the title of the window, you can use the *figure* function that we already know.

```
plt.figure("MyFigure")
```

LABELING AXES

As a next step, we are going to label our axes. For this, we use the two functions *xlabel* and *ylabel*.

```
plt.xlabel("x-values")
plt.ylabel("y-values")
```

You can choose whatever labels you like. When we combine all these pieces of code, we end up with a graph like this:

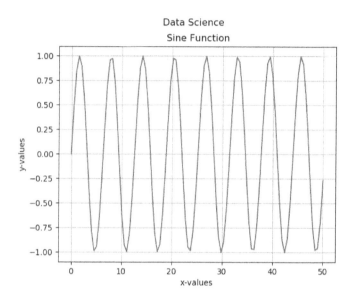

In this case, the labels aren't really necessary because it is obvious what we see here. But sometimes we want to describe what our values actually mean and what the plot is about.

LEGENDS

Sometimes we will have multiple graphs and objects in a plot. We then use legends to label these individual elements, in order to make everything more readable.

```
x = np.linspace(10,50,100)
y1 = np.sin(x)
y2 = np.cos(x)
y3 = np.log(x/3)

plt.plot(x,y1,'b-',label="Sine")
plt.plot(x,y2,'r-',label="Cosine")
plt.plot(x,y3,'g-',label="Logarithm")

plt.legend(loc='upper left')

plt.show()
```

Here we have three functions, *sine*, *cosine* and a *logarithmic* function. We draw all graphs into one plot and add a label to them. In order to make these labels visible, we then use the function *legend* and specify a location for it. Here we chose the *upper left*. Our result looks like this:

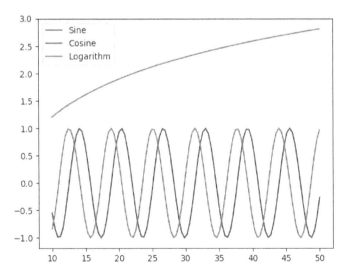

As you can see, the legend makes our plot way more readable and it also looks more professional.

Saving Diagrams

So now that we know quite a lot about plotting and graphing, let's take a look at how to save our diagrams.

```
plt.savefig("functions.png")
```

Actually, this is quite simple. We just plot whatever we want to plot and then use the function *savefig* to save our figure into an image file.

5 – Matplotlib Plot Types

In the last chapter, we mainly plotted functions and a couple of values. But Matplotlib offers a huge arsenal of different plot types. Here we are going to take a look at these.

Histograms

Let's start out with some statistics here. So-called *histograms* represent the distribution of numerical values. For example, we could graph the distribution of heights amongst students in a class.

```
mu, sigma = 172, 4
x = mu + sigma * np.random.randn(10000)
```

We start by defining a mean value *mu* (average height) and a standard deviation *sigma*. To create our x-values, we use our *mu* and *sigma* combined with 10000 randomly generated values. Notice that we are using the *randn* function here. This function generates values for a *standard normal distribution*, which means that we will get a bell curve of values.

```
plt.hist(x, 100, density=True, facecolor="blue")
```

Then we use the *hist* function, in order to plot our histogram. The second parameter states how many values we want to plot. Also, we want our values to be normed. So we set the parameter *density* to *True*. This means that our y-values will sum up to one and we can view them as percentages. Last but not least, we set the color to blue.

Now, when we show this plot, we will realize that it is a bit confusing. So we are going to add some labeling here.

```
plt.xlabel("Height")
plt.ylabel("Probability")
plt.title("Height of Students")
plt.text(160, 0.125,"μ = 172, σ = 4")
plt.axis([155,190,0,0.15])
plt.grid(True)
```

First we label the two axes. The x-values represent the height of the students, whereas the y-values represent the probability that a randomly picked student has the respective height. Besides the title, we also add some text to our graph. We place it at the x-value 160 and the y-value of 0.125. The text just states the values for μ (mu) and σ (sigma). Last but not least, we set the ranges for the two axes. Our x-values range from 155 to 190 and our y-values from 0 to 0.15. Also, the grid is turned on. This is what our graph looks like at the end:

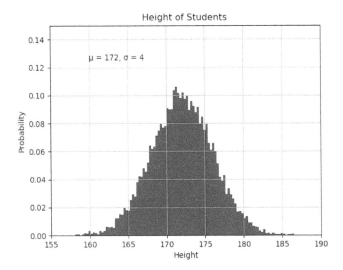

We can see the Gaussian bell curve which is typical for the standard normal distribution.

BAR CHART

For visualizing certain statistics, *bar charts* are oftentimes very useful, especially when it comes to categories. In our case, we are going to plot the skill levels of three different people in the IT realm.

```
bob = (90, 67, 87, 76)
charles = (80, 80, 47, 66)
daniel = (40, 95, 76, 89)

skills = ("Python", "Java", "Networking",
"Machine Learning")
```

Here we have the three persons *Bob, Charles* and *Daniel*. They are represented by tuples with four values that indicate their skill levels in Python programming, Java programming, networking and machine learning.

```
width = 0.2
index = np.arange(4)
plt.bar(index, bob,
        width=width, label="Bob")
plt.bar(index + width, charles,
        width=width, label="Charles")
plt.bar(index + width * 2, daniel,
        width=width, label="Daniel")
```

We then use the *bar* function to plot our bar chart. For this, we define an array with the indices one to four and a bar width of 0.2. For each person we plot the four respective values and label them.

```
plt.xticks(index + width, skills)
plt.ylim(0,120)
plt.title("IT Skill Levels")
plt.ylabel("Skill Level")
plt.xlabel("IT Skill")
plt.legend()
```

Then we label the x-ticks with the method *xticks* and set the limit of the y-axis to 120 to free up some space for our legend. After that we set a title and label the axes. The result looks like this:

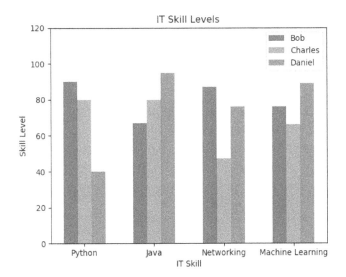

We can now see who is the most skilled in each category. Of course we could also change the graph so that we have the persons on the x-axis with the skill-colors in the legend.

PIE CHART

Pie charts are used to display proportions of numbers. For example, we could graph how many percent of the students have which nationality.

```
labels = ('American', 'German', 'French',
'Other')
values = (47, 23, 20, 10)
```

We have one tuple with our four nationalities. They will be our labels. And we also have one tuple with the percentages.

```
plt.pie(values, labels=labels,
        autopct="%.2f%%", shadow=True)
plt.title("Student Nationalities")

plt.show()
```

Now we just need to use the *pie* function, to draw our chart. We pass our values and our labels. Then we set the *autopct* parameter to our desired percentage format. Also, we turn on the *shadow* of the chart and set a title. And this is what we end up with:

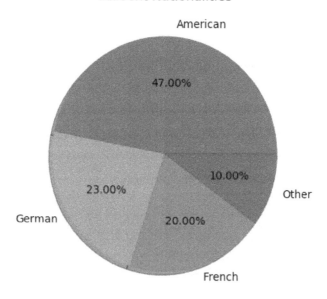

As you can see, this chart is perfect for visualizing percentages.

SCATTER PLOTS

So-called *scatter plots* are used to represent two-dimensional data using dots.

```
x = np.random.rand(50)
y = np.random.rand(50)

plt.scatter(x,y)

plt.show()
```

Here we just generate 50 random x-values and 50 random y-values. By using the *scatter* function, we can then plot them.

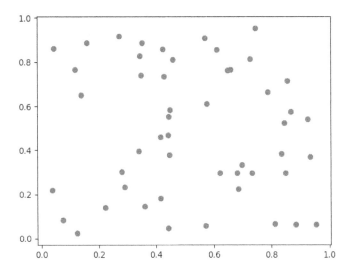

BOXPLOT

Boxplot diagrams are used, in order to split data into *quartiles*. We do that to get information about the distribution of our values. The question we want to answer is: How widely spread is the data in each of the quartiles.

```
mu, sigma = 172, 4
values = np.random.normal(mu,sigma,200)

plt.boxplot(values)
plt.title("Student's Height")
plt.ylabel("Height")
plt.show()
```

In this example, we again create a normal distribution of the heights of our students. Our mean value is 172, our standard deviation 4 and we generate 200 values. Then we plot our boxplot diagram.

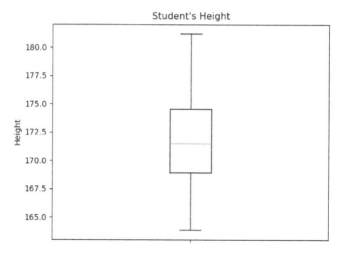

Here we see the result. Notice that a boxplot doesn't give information about the frequency of the individual values. It only gives information about the spread of the values in the individual quartiles. Every quartile has 25% of the values but some have a very small spread whereas others have quite a large one.

3D PLOTS

Now last but not least, let's take a look at 3D-plotting. For this, we will need to import another plotting module. It is called *mpl_toolkits* and it is part of the Matplotlib stack.

```
from mpl_toolkits import mplot3d
```

Specifically, we import the module *mplot3d* from this library. Then, we can use *3d* as a parameter when defining our axes.

```
ax = plt.axes(projection='3d')
plt.show()
```

We can only use this parameter, when *mplot3d* is imported. Now, our plot looks like this:

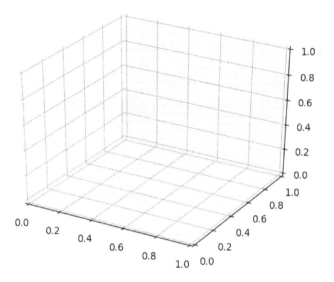

Since we are now plotting in three dimensions, we will also need to define three axes.

```
z = np.linspace(0, 20, 100)
x = np.sin(z)
y = np.cos(z)

ax = plt.axes(projection='3d')
ax.plot3D(x,y,z)
plt.show()
```

In this case, we are taking the z-axis as the input. The z-axis is the one which goes upwards. We define the x-axis and the y-axis to be a sine and cosine function. Then, we use the function *plot3D* to plot our function. We end up with this:

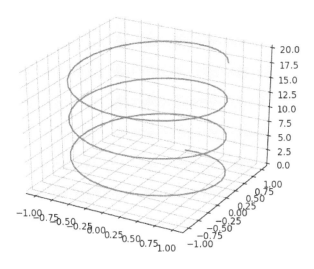

SURFACE PLOTS

Now in order to plot a function with a surface, we need to calculate every point on it. This is impossible, which is why we are just going to calculate enough to estimate the graph. In this case, x and y will be the input and the z-function will be the 3D-result which is composed of them.

```python
ax = plt.axes(projection='3d')

def z_function(x, y):
    return np.sin(np.sqrt(x ** 2 + y ** 2))

x = np.linspace(-5, 5, 50)
y = np.linspace(-5, 5, 50)
```

We start by defining a *z_function* which is a combination of sine, square root and squaring the input. Our inputs are just 50 numbers from -5 to 5.

```
X, Y = np.meshgrid(x,y)
Z = z_function(X,Y)

ax.plot_surface(X,Y,Z)
plt.show()
```

Then we define new variables for x and y (we are using capitals this time). What we do is converting the x- and y-vectors into matrices using the *meshgrid* function. Finally, we use the *z_function* to calculate our z-values and then we plot our surface by using the method *plot_surface*. This is the result:

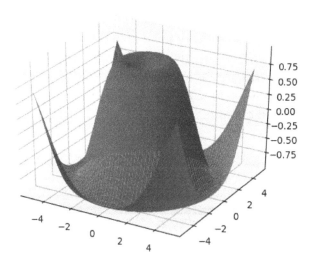

Play around with these charts and plots until you really understand them. Visualizing functions and data is very important in data science.

6 – PANDAS DATA ANALYSIS

Pandas is probably the most powerful libraries of this book. It provides high-performance tools for data manipulation and analysis. Furthermore, it is very effective at converting data formats and querying data out of databases. The two main data structures of Pandas are the *series* and the *data frame.* To work with Pandas, we need to import the module.

```
import pandas as pd
```

PANDAS SERIES

A series in Pandas is a one-dimensional array which is labeled. You can imagine it to be the data science equivalent of an ordinary Python dictionary.

```
series = pd.Series([10, 20, 30, 40],
                   ['A', 'B', 'C', 'D'])
```

In order to create a series, we use the constructor of the *Series* class. The first parameter that we pass is a list full of values (in this case numbers). The second parameter is the list of the indices or keys (in this case strings). When we now print our series, we can see what the structure looks like.

```
A    10
B    20
C    30
D    40
dtype: int64
```

The first column represents the indices, whereas the second column represents the actual values.

ACCESSING VALUES

The accessing of values works in the same way that it works with dictionaries. We need to address the respective index or key to get our desired value.

```
print(series['C'])
print(series[1])
```

As you can see, we can choose how we want to access our elements. We can either address the key or the position that the respective element is at.

CONVERTING DICTIONARIES

Since series and dictionaries are quite similar, we can easily convert our Python dictionaries into Pandas series.

```
myDict = {'A':10, 'B':20, 'C':30}
series = pd.Series(myDict)
```

Now the keys are our indices and the values remain values. But what we can also do is, to change the order of the indices.

```
myDict = {'A':10, 'B':20, 'C':30}
series = pd.Series(myDict,
index=['C','A','B'])
```

Our series now looks like this:

```
C       30
A       10
B       20
dtype: int64
```

PANDAS DATA FRAME

In contrast to the series, a data frame is not one-dimensional but multi-dimensional and looks like a table. You can imagine it to be like an Excel table or a data base table.

```
data = {'Name': ['Anna', 'Bob', 'Charles'],
        'Age': [24, 32, 35],
        'Height': [176, 187, 175]}

df = pd.DataFrame(data)
```

To create a Pandas data frame, we use the constructor of the class. In this case, we first create a dictionary with some data about three persons. We feed that data into our data frame. It then looks like this:

```
      Name  Age  Height
0     Anna   24     176
1      Bob   32     187
2  Charles   35     175
```

As you can see, without any manual work, we already have a structured data frame and table.

To now access the values is a bit more complicated than with series. We have multiple columns and multiple rows, so we need to address two values.

```
print(df['Name'][1])
```

So first we choose the column *Name* and then we choose the second element (index one) of this column. In this case, this is *Bob*.

When we omit the last index, we can also select only the one column. This is useful when we want to save specific columns of our data frame into a new one. What we can also do in this case is to select multiple columns.

```
print(df[['Name', 'Height']])
```

Here we select two columns by addressing a list of two strings. The result is the following:

```
     Name  Height
0    Anna     176
1     Bob     187
2  Charles     175
```

DATA FRAME FUNCTIONS

Now, let us get a little bit more into the functions of a data frame.

BASIC FUNCTIONS AND ATTRIBUTES

For data frames we have a couple of basic functions and attributes that we already know from lists or NumPy arrays.

BASIC FUNCTIONS AND ATTRIBUTES	
FUNCTION	**DESCRIPTION**
df.T	Transposes the rows and columns of the data frame
df.dtypes	Returns data types of the data frame
df.ndim	Returns the number of dimensions of the data frame
df.shape	Returns the shape of the data frame
df.size	Returns the number of elements in the data frame
df.head(n)	Returns the first n rows of the data frame (default is five)
df.tail(n)	Returns the last n rows of the data frame (default is five)

STATISTICAL FUNCTIONS

For the statistical functions, we will now extend our data frame a little bit and add some more persons.

```
data = {'Name': ['Anna', 'Bob', 'Charles',
                 'Daniel', 'Evan', 'Fiona',
                 'Gerald', 'Henry',
'India'],
        'Age':
[24,32,35,45,22,54,55,43,25],
        'Height': [176,187,175,182,176,
                   189,165,187,167]}

df = pd.DataFrame(data)
```

STATISTICAL FUNCTIONS	
FUNCTION	**DESCRIPTION**
count()	Count the number of non-null elements
sum()	Returns the sum of values of the selected columns
mean()	Returns the arithmetic mean of values of the selected columns
median()	Returns the median of values of the selected columns
mode()	Returns the value that occurs most often in the columns selected
std()	Returns standard deviation of the values
min()	Returns the minimum value

max()	Returns the maximum value
abs()	Returns the absolute values of the elements
prod()	Returns the product of the selected elements
describe()	Returns data frame with all statistical values summarized

Now, we are not going to dig deep into every single function here. But let's take a look at how to apply some of them.

```
print(df['Age'].mean())
print(df['Height'].median())
```

Here we choose a column and then apply the statistical functions on it. What we get is just a single scalar with the desired value.

```
37.22222222222222
176.0
```

We can also apply the functions to the whole data frame. In this case, we get returned another data frame with the results for each column.

```
print(df.mean())
```

```
Age        37.222222
Height    178.222222
dtype: float64
```

APPLYING NUMPY FUNCTIONS

Instead of using the built-in Pandas functions, we can also use the methods we already know. For this, we just use the *apply* function of the data frame and then pass our desired method.

```
print(df['Age'].apply(np.sin))
```

In this example, we apply the sine function onto our ages. It doesn't make any sense but it demonstrates how this works.

LAMBDA EXPRESSIONS

A very powerful in Python are *lambda expression*. They can be thought of as nameless functions that we pass as a parameter.

```
print(df['Age'].apply(lambda x: x * 100))
```

By using the keyword *lambda* we create a temporary variable that represents the individual values that we are applying the operation onto. After the colon, we define what we want to do. In this case, we multiply all values of the column *Age* by 100.

```
df = df[['Age', 'Height']]

print(df.apply(lambda x: x.max() -
x.min()))
```

Here we removed the *Name* column, so that we only have numerical values. Since we are applying our expression on the whole data frame now, *x* refers to the whole columns. What we do here is calculating the difference between the maximum value and the minimum value.

```
Age       33
Height    24
dtype: int64
```

The oldest and the youngest are 33 years apart and the tallest and the tiniest are 24 centimeters apart.

ITERATING

Iterating over data frames is quite easy with Pandas. We can either do it in the classic way or use specific functions for it.

```
for x in df['Age']:
    print(x)
```

As you can see, iterating over a column's value is very simple and nothing new. This would print all the ages. When we iterate over the whole data frame, our control variable takes on the column names.

STATISTICAL FUNCTIONS	
FUNCTION	**DESCRIPTION**
iteritems()	Iterator for key-value pairs
iterrows()	Iterator for the rows (index, series)
itertuples()	Iterator for the rows as named tuples

Let's take a look at some practical examples.

```
for key, value in df.iteritems():
    print("{}: {}".format(key, value))
```

Here we use the *iteritems* function to iterate over key-value pairs. What we get is a huge output of all rows for each column.

On the other hand, when we use *iterrows*, we can print out all the column-values for each row or index.

```
for index, value in df.iterrows():
    print(index,value)
```

We get packages like this one for every index:

```
0 Name        Anna
Age          24
Height       176
Name: 0, dtype: object
```

Sorting

One very powerful thing about Pandas data frames is that we can easily sort them.

Sort by Index

```
df = pd.DataFrame(np.random.rand(10,2),

index=[1,5,3,6,7,2,8,9,0,4],
                  columns=['A','B'])
```

Here we create a new data frame, which is filled with random numbers. We specify our own indices and as you can see, they are completely unordered.

```
print(df.sort_index())
```

By using the method *sort_index*, we sort the whole data frame by the index column. The result is now sorted:

```
          A         B
0   0.193432  0.514303
1   0.391481  0.193495
2   0.159516  0.607314
3   0.273120  0.056247
...       ...       ...
```

Inplace Parameter

When we use functions that manipulate our data frame, we don't actually change it but we return a manipulated copy. If we wanted to apply the changes on the actual data frame, we would need to do it like this:

```
df = df.sort_index()
```

But Pandas offers us another alternative as well. This alternative is the parameter *inplace*. When this parameter is set to *True*, the changes get applied to our actual data frame.

```
df.sort_index(inplace=True)
```

SORT BY COLUMNS

Now, we can also sort our data frame by specific columns.

```
data = {'Name': ['Anna', 'Bob', 'Charles',
                 'Daniel', 'Evan', 'Fiona',
                 'Gerald', 'Henry',
'India'],
        'Age':
[24,24,35,45,22,54,54,43,25],
        'Height': [176,187,175,182,176,
                   189,165,187,167]}

df = pd.DataFrame(data)

df.sort_values(by=['Age', 'Height'],
               inplace=True)

print(df)
```

Here we have our old data frame slightly modified. We use the function *sort_values* to sort our data frames. The parameter *by* states the columns that we are sorting by. In this case, we are first sorting by age and if two persons have the same age, we sort by height.

JOINING AND MERGING

Another powerful concept in Pandas is *joining* and *merging* data frames.

```
names = pd.DataFrame({
    'id': [1,2,3,4,5],
    'name': ['Anna', 'Bob', 'Charles',
             'Daniel', 'Evan'],
})

ages = pd.DataFrame({
    'id': [1,2,3,4,5],
    'age': [20,30,40,50,60]
})
```

Now when we have two separate data frames which are related to one another, we can combine them into one data frame. It is important that we have a common column that we can merge on. In this case, this is *id*.

```
df = pd.merge(names,ages,on='id')
df.set_index('id', inplace=True)
```

First we use the method *merge* and specify the column to merge on. We then have a new data frame with the combined data but we also want our *id* column to be the index. For this, we use the *set_index* method.

The result looks like this:

```
     name   age
id
1      Anna   20
2       Bob   30
3   Charles   40
4    Daniel   50
5      Evan   60
```

JOINS

It is not necessarily always obvious *how* we want to merge our data frames. This is where *joins* come into play. We have four types of joins.

JOIN MERGE TYPES	
JOIN	**DESCRIPTION**
left	Uses all keys from left object and merges with right
right	Uses all keys from right object and merges with left
outer	Uses all keys from both objects and merges them
inner	Uses only the keys which both objects have and merges them (default)

Now let's change our two data frames a little bit.

```
names = pd.DataFrame({
    'id': [1,2,3,4,5,6],
    'name': ['Anna', 'Bob', 'Charles',
             'Daniel', 'Evan', 'Fiona'],
})
```

```
ages = pd.DataFrame({
    'id': [1,2,3,4,5,7],
    'age': [20,30,40,50,60,70]
})
```

Our *names* frame now has an additional index *6* and an additional name. And our *ages* frame has an additional index *7* with an additional name.

```
df = pd.merge(names,ages,on='id',
how='inner')
df.set_index('id', inplace=True)
```

If we now perform the default *inner join*, we will end up with the same data frame as in the beginning. We only take the keys which both objects have. This means one to five.

```
df = pd.merge(names,ages,on='id',
how='left')
df.set_index('id', inplace=True)
```

When we use the *left join*, we get all the keys from the *names* data frame but not the additional index *7* from ages. This also means that *Fiona* won't be assigned any age.

```
        name    age
id
1       Anna    20.0
2        Bob    30.0
3    Charles    40.0
4     Daniel    50.0
5       Evan    60.0
6      Fiona    NaN
```

The same principle goes for the *right join* just the other way around.

```
df = pd.merge(names,ages,on='id',
how='right')
df.set_index('id', inplace=True)
```

```
        name  age
id
1       Anna   20
2        Bob   30
3    Charles   40
4     Daniel   50
5       Evan   60
7        NaN   70
```

Now, we only have the keys from the *ages* frame and the *6* is missing. Finally, if we use the *outer join*, we combine all keys into one data frame.

```
df = pd.merge(names,ages,on='id',
how='outer')
df.set_index('id', inplace=True)
```

```
        name   age
id
1       Anna  20.0
2        Bob  30.0
3    Charles  40.0
4     Daniel  50.0
5       Evan  60.0
6      Fiona   NaN
7        NaN  70.0
```

QUERYING DATA

Like in databases with SQL, we can also query data from our data frames in Pandas. For this, we use the function *loc*, in which we put our expression.

```
print(df.loc[df['Age'] == 24])
print(df.loc[(df['Age'] == 24) &
             (df['Height'] > 180)])
print(df.loc[df['Age'] > 30]['Name'])
```

Here we have some good examples to explain how this works. The first expression returns all rows where the value for *Age* is 24.

```
    Name   Age   Height
0   Anna    24      176
1    Bob    24      187
```

The second query is a bit more complicated. Here we combine two conditions. The first one is that the age needs to be 24 but we then combine this with the condition that the height is greater than 180. This leaves us with one row.

```
   Name   Age   Height
1   Bob    24      187
```

In the last expression, we can see that we are only choosing one column to be returned. We want the names of all people that are older than 30.

```
2     Charles
3      Daniel
5       Fiona
6      Gerald
7       Henry
```

READ DATA FROM FILES

Similar to NumPy, we can also easily read data from external files into Pandas. Let's say we have an CSV-File like this (opened in Excel):

	A	B	C	D
1	id	name	age	height
2		1 Anna	20	178
3		2 Bob	30	172
4		3 Charles	40	189
5		4 Daniel	50	192
6		5 Evan	60	183
7		6 Fiona	70	165
8				

The only thing that we need to do now is to use the function *read_csv* to import our data into a data frame.

```
df = pd.read_csv('data.csv')
df.set_index('id', inplace=True)
print(df)
```

We also set the index to the *id* column again. This is what we have imported:

```
       name  age  height
id
1      Anna   20     178
2       Bob   30     172
3   Charles   40     189
4    Daniel   50     192
5      Evan   60     183
6     Fiona   70     165
```

This of course, also works the other way around. By using the method *to_csv*, we can also save our data frame into a CSV-file.

```
data = {'Name': ['Anna', 'Bob', 'Charles',
                 'Daniel', 'Evan', 'Fiona',
                 'Gerald', 'Henry',
'India'],
        'Age':
[24,24,35,45,22,54,54,43,25],
        'Height': [176,187,175,182,176,
                   189,165,187,167]}

df = pd.DataFrame(data)
df.to_csv('mydf.csv')
```

Then we have this CSV-file (opened in Excel):

	A	B	C	D
1		Name	Age	Height
2		0 Anna	24	176
3		1 Bob	24	187
4		2 Charles	35	175
5		3 Daniel	45	182
6		4 Evan	22	176
7		5 Fiona	54	189
8		6 Gerald	54	165
9		7 Henry	43	187
10		8 India	25	167
11				

PLOTTING DATA

Since Pandas builds on Matplotlib, we can easily visualize the data from our data frame.

```
data = {'Name': ['Anna', 'Bob', 'Charles',
                 'Daniel', 'Evan', 'Fiona',
                 'Gerald', 'Henry',
'India'],
        'Age':
[24,24,35,45,22,54,54,43,25],
        'Height': [176,187,175,182,176,
                   189,165,187,167]}

df = pd.DataFrame(data)
df.sort_values(by=['Age', 'Height'])
df.hist()
plt.show()
```

In this example, we use the method *hist* to plot a histogram of our numerical columns. Without specifying anything more, this is what we end up with:

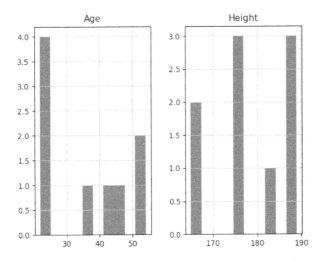

But we can also just use the function *plot* to plot our data frame or individual columns.

```
df.plot()
plt.show()
```

The result is the following:

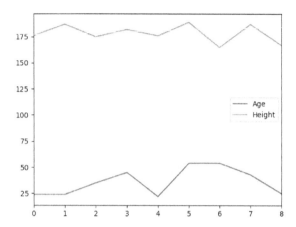

Of course we can also just use the Matplotlib library itself and pass the columns as parameters.

```
plt.plot(df['Age'], 'bo')
plt.show()
```

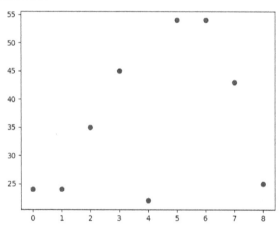

WHAT'S NEXT?

Finally, we are done with the third volume of the Python Bible series. It was very practical and went deep into the topic of data science. This has now laid the foundation for more complex topics like machine learning and finance, which will be the follow-ups to this book. You are on a very good path! Just make sure you practice everything until you really understand the material that we talked about.

You are now definitely able to find some huge data sets online (maybe in CSV-format) and analyze them with Python. And I encourage you to do that. We only learn by doing and practicing. In the next volumes we will also import data from online sources and APIs. And we are not only going to analyze this data but also to make predictions with it.

Now that you've read the first three volumes of this series, I encourage you to continue on this journey because it is NOW that things get really interesting. I hope you could get some value out of this book and that it helped you to become a better programmer. So stay tuned and prepare for the next volume!

Last but not least, a little reminder. This book was written for you, so that you can get as much value as possible and learn to code effectively. If you find this book valuable or you think you learned something new, please write a quick review on Amazon. It is completely free and takes about one minute. But it helps me produce more high quality books, which you can benefit from.

Thank you!

If this trilogy benefited your programming life and you think that you have learned something valuable, please consider a quick review on Amazon.

Thank you!

NeuralNine

If you are interested in free educational content about programming and machine learning, check out https://www.neuralnine.com/

There we have free blog posts, videos and more for you! Also, you can follow the ***@neuralnine*** Instagram account for daily infographics about programming and AI!

Website: https://www.neuralnine.com/

Instagram: @neuralnine

YouTube: NeuralNine

www.ingramcontent.com/pod-product-compliance
Lightning Source LLC
Chambersburg PA
CBHW051232050326
40689CB00007B/887